Internet

by Ned Snell

A Division of Macmillan Computer Publishing
201 W. 103rd Street, Indianapolis, Indiana 46290 USA

Internet Cheat Sheet

Copyright © 1999 by Que Corporation

International Standard Book Number: 0-7897-1845-6

Library of Congress Catalog Card Number: 98-86863

Printed in the United States of America

First Printing: 1999

00   4

Interpretation of the printing code: the rightmost number of the first series of numbers is the year of the book's printing; the rightmost number of the second series of numbers is the number of the book's printing. For example, a printing code of 99-1 shows that the first printing of the book occurred in 1999.

Trademarks

Executive Editor	*Jim Minatel*
Acquisitions Editor	*Don Essig*
Development Editor	*Lisa Wagner*
Managing Editor	*Thomas Hayes*
Project Editor	*Lori A. Lyons*
Copy Editor	*Julie McNamee*
Technical Editor	*David Garratt*
Indexer	*Lisa Stumpf*
Proofreader	*Jeanne Clark*
Production	*Steve Geiselman*

Contents

Part 2 Browsing the Web

Part 3   Making Your Browser Do More

Part 4 Finding Web Sites

Part 5 Finding Other Stuff

Part 6 Exchanging Email

Part 7 Joining a Discussion

Part 8 Live Communication

Part 9 Making the Most of the Internet

Part 10 Your Very Own Web Page

Tell Us What You Think!

As the reader of this book, *you* are our most important critic and commentator. We value your opinion and want to know what we're doing right, what we could do better, what areas you'd like to see us publish in, and any other words of wisdom you're willing to pass our way.

As the Executive Editor for the General Desktop Applications team at Macmillan Computer Publishing, I welcome your comments. You can fax, email, or write me directly to let me know what you did or didn't like about this book—as well as what we can do to make our books stronger.

Please note that I cannot help you with technical problems related to the topic of this book, and that due to the high volume of mail I receive, I might not be able to reply to every message.

When you write, please be sure to include this book's title and author as well as your name and phone or fax number. I will carefully review your comments and share them with the author and editors who worked on the book.

Fax: 317-817-7070

Email: internet@mcp.com

Mail: Executive Editor
         General Desktop Applications
         Macmillan Computer Publishing
         201 West 103rd Street
         Indianapolis, IN 46290 USA

Introduction

You're eager to get on the Internet, but you want doing so made quick and easy, right? You're in the right place.

In a moment, you'll begin making quick, easy work of getting onto and all around the Internet. I'll wrap up this Introduction in a snap so that you can get started!

What's Unique About This Book?

As you go along, you'll notice a variety of features in this book designed to help you learn to use the Internet as quickly and easily as possible:

- **Headings** appear in the left margin of each page, to help you quickly find (or skip!) information.

- **Step-by-step** instructions lead you through tasks, where appropriate.

- **Pictures** show you what's going on.

- **Highlighting** calls your attention to important ideas or steps.

- A **Cheat Sheet** at the start of each chapter gives a quick rundown of the concepts and activities you'll explore.

- **Basic Survival** sections come first in each chapter, giving you quick access to the most basic, essential material.

- **Beyond Survival** sections follow, showing more advanced (and optional) activities—still explored in an easy-to-understand fashion.

- **Hand-Written Tips** in the margin offer advice, warnings, or alternative ways of accomplishing the task at hand.

Who Should Read This Book?

This book is *system neutral*, which is another way of saying you can use this book no matter what kind of computer you have. Don't have a computer yet? In Chapter 2, I'll help you choose one that's properly equipped for the Net.

As you'll see, using the Internet is pretty much the same no matter what computer you use it from. Setting up each type of computer for the Internet is a little different, however, so I help you set up a PC or a Mac for the Internet in Part 1.

You do not need to know a thing about the Internet, computer networks, or any of that stuff to get started with this book. However, you do need to know your way around your own computer. With a basic, everyday ability to operate the type of computer from which you will use the Internet, you're ready to begin. I'll take you the rest of the way.

How to Use This Book

This book is divided into ten parts:

> **Part 1** introduces you to the Net and the many different things you can do there, and shows you how to get yourself and your computer set up for it.
>
> **Part 2** takes you onto the World Wide Web, the fun, graphical, incredibly useful part of the Net that everybody's talking about.
>
> **Part 3** shows how to soup up your Web browser program (such as Internet Explorer or Netscape Navigator) so that it can do more.
>
> **Part 4** shows how to find Web sites covering a topic you want to learn more about: a product, company, hobby, and so on.
>
> **Part 5** shows how to search for other stuff (besides Web sites) on the Net, such as free software or the email addresses and phone numbers of friends.

Part 6 covers exchanging email messages with anyone on the Internet—and how to stop annoying junk email.

Part 7 shows how to join and contribute to two kinds of Internet-based discussion groups: mailing lists and newsgroups.

Part 8 shows the ways you can communicate "live" with others on the Internet, such as joining an online chat or having a voice/video conference.

Part 9 offers a grab-bag of ways to get more from the Net (and to do so safely), such as making the Internet safe for your kids or buying and selling online.

Part 10 shows how you can create and publish your very own Web pages so that anyone on the Internet can visit. Part 10 also shows you how to create email messages that are as fancy as any Web page, containing pictures and cool typography.

Three appendixes contain information that's potentially useful and absolutely optional:

Appendix A offers up an easy-to-use directory of Web pages I think you might enjoy visiting.

Appendix B shows where and how to pick up any of the latest and greatest Internet software.

Appendix C tells you what to do when (if) your Net travels don't go the way you expect them to.

As you can see, the parts move logically from setting up for the Net to using it, and from easy stuff to not-so-easy stuff.

Acknowledgments

Many folks helped with this book, but the following deserve special praise for its fine design and execution:

My family
Lisa Swayne
Don Essig
Maxine London

PART

1

Getting Started

In many ways, the Internet today is a pretty self-explanatory place to be—after you get there. For many folks, the hardest part of the Internet—the only hard part, really—is getting set up for it. This part of the book makes setting up and getting connected simple. You pick up such start-up essentials as

- Understanding the Internet
- What Hardware Do You Need?
- What Software Do You Need?
- About Internet Accounts
- Choosing an Internet Provider or Online Service
- Connecting to the Internet

Cheat Sheet

What's the Net?

The Internet is a global network of computers, interconnected so they can exchange information.

Knowing Your Condition: Online or Offline

When you're actively connected to the Internet, you're *online*. When you're not, you're *offline*. Information or other resources that can be accessed through the Net are also described as online resources.

What Can You Do Through the Net?

Using the Web, you can access Web pages from which you can

- Visit companies, governments, museums, schools, and other organizations.
- Read the news from major and minor media.
- Explore public and private libraries.
- Read books and magazines.
- Get software to use on your computer.
- Shop for stuff.
- Play games, watch a video, get a degree, waste time…

Understanding Clients and Server

The information and messages on the Net are stored in computers called servers—Web servers, email servers, and so on. Each type of server can be accessed only by its own kind of client program, so you need an email program for email, a Web browser for the Web, and so on.

What Else Can You Do Through the Net?

- Exchange messages via email.
- Have a discussion on a given topic, through messages posted on a mailing list or newsgroup.
- Exchange "live" messages with others in a Chat session.
- Have a live voice or video conference.

Understanding the Internet

You probably think you already know what the Internet is, and you're probably 90% right, for all practical purposes. But by developing just a little better understanding of what the Net's all about, you'll find learning to use it much easier.

Basic Survival

What's the Net?

A computer network today can be as small as two PCs hooked together in an office, and it can be as big as thousands of computers of all different types spread all over the world and connected to one another not just by wires, but through telephone lines and even through the air via satellite.

To build a really big network, you build lots of little networks and then hook the networks to each other, creating an *internetwork*. That's all the Internet really is: The world's largest internetwork (hence its name).

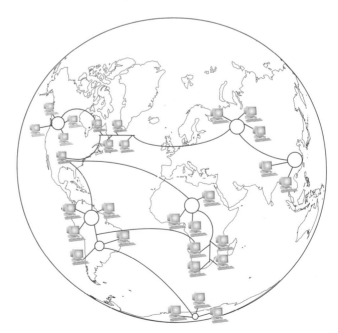

In homes, businesses, schools, and government offices all over the world, millions of computers of all different types—PCs, Macintoshes, big corporate mainframes, and others—are connected together in networks. Those networks are connected to one another to form the Internet.

Knowing Your Condition: Online or Offline

When your computer has a live, open connection to the Internet enabling you to do something, you and your computer are said to be online. When the Internet connection is closed (because your computer is off or for any other reason), you're offline.

The idea is easier to grasp if you think in telephone terms: When you're on a call (even if nobody's talking), you're online; when the phone's in its cradle, you're offline.

What Can You Do Through the Net?

It's likely that your interest in the Internet was sparked by something called the World Wide Web, even if you don't know it. When you see news stories about the Internet showing someone looking at a cool, colorful screen full of things to see and do, that person is looking at the World Wide Web, commonly called "the Web."

The Web is sometimes also referred to as "WWW."

All those funky looking Internet addresses you see in ads today—www.pepsi.com and so forth—are the addresses you need to visit companies on the Web. With an Internet connection and a Web browser program—such as Internet Explorer or Netscape Navigator—on your computer, you can type an address to visit a particular Web site and read the Web pages stored there.

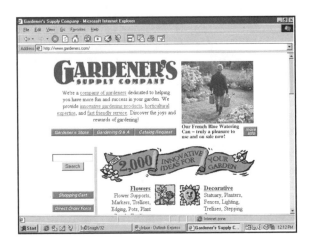

Browsing = using a Web browsing program to explore the Web.

By browsing the Web, you can do a staggering number of different things, including all of the following:

Visit Companies, Governments, Museums, Schools

Just about any large organization has its own Web site these days. Many smaller organizations have their own sites, too. You can visit these sites to learn more about products you want to buy, school or government policies, and much more.

For example, I belong to an HMO for medical coverage. I can visit my HMO's Web site to find and choose a new doctor, review policy restrictions, and much more. Just as easily, I can check out tax rules or order forms on the Internal Revenue Service Web site. I can also view paintings in museums all over the world, or find out when the next Parent's Night is at the local elementary school.

Read the News

Better Web news sites are more up-to-the-minute than even TV or radio news.

CNN has its own Web site, as do the *New York Times*, the *Wall Street Journal*, and dozens of other media outlets ranging from major print magazines, to fly-by-night rags spreading rumors, to small sites featuring news about any imaginable topic. You'll also find a number of great news sources that have no print or broadcast counterpart—they're exclusive to the Web.

Whatever kind of news you prefer, you can find it on the Web. Unlike most broadcast news, you can look at Web news any time you find convenient.

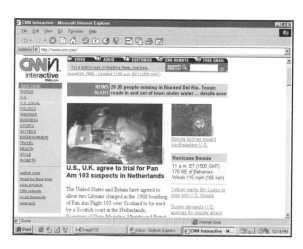

Explore Libraries

Some libraries even let you borrow online.

Many libraries, large and small, are making their catalogs available online. That means I can find out which of the dozen libraries I use has the book I need, without spending a day driving to each.

Read

Books are published right on the Web, including classics (Shakespeare, Dickens) and new works. You can read them right on your screen, or print them out to read later on the bus. The Web has even initiated its own kind of literature, collaborative fiction, in which visitors to a Web site can read—and contribute to—a story in progress.

Shop

One of the fastest-growing, and most controversial, Web activities is shopping. Right on the Web, you can browse an online catalog, choose merchandise, type in a credit card number and shipping address, and receive your merchandise in a few days, postage paid. Besides merchandise, you can buy just about anything else on the Web: stocks, legal services, you name it. Everything but surgery, and I'm sure that's only a matter of time.

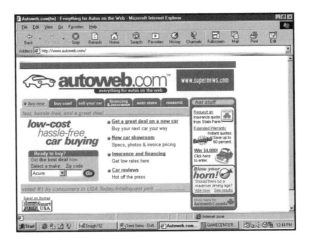

Get Software

Because computer software can travel through the Internet, you can actually get software right through the Web and use it on your PC. Some of the software is free, some isn't. But it's all there, whenever you need it—no box, no CD, no problem.

Play Games, Watch Videos, Get a Degree, Waste Time

Have I left anything out? There's too much on the Web to cover succinctly. But I hope you get the idea. The Web is where it's at.

Beyond Survival

Most of the information you will access through the Internet is stored on computers called servers. A server can be any type of computer; what makes it a server is the role it plays. It stores information for use by clients.

A client is a computer—or, more accurately, a particular computer program—that knows how to communicate with a particular type of server to use information stored on that server (or to put information there). For example, when you surf the Web, you use a client program called a Web browser—such as Netscape Navigator or Internet Explorer—to communicate with a computer where Web pages are stored—a Web server.

In general, each type of Internet activity involves a different type of client and server: To use the Web, you need a Web browser to communicate with Web servers. To use email, you need an email program—or email client—to communicate with email servers.

Appendix B, "Popular Internet Software and Where to Get It," shows where to get great Internet software online.

Understanding Clients and Server

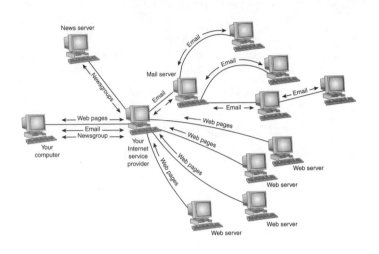

What *Else* Can You Do Through the Net?

Again, the main attraction to the Internet is the Web. If you get an Internet account (as described in Chapters 4, "About Internet Accounts," and 5, "Choosing an Internet Provider or Online Service"), however, you can do much more, all of which you learn to do in this book.

Exchange Messages

An *email*, in case you didn't know, is a message sent as an electronic file from one computer to another. Using Internet email, you can type a message on your computer and send it to anyone else on the Internet.

Each user on the Internet has a unique email address; if your email address is suzyq@netknow.com, you're the only person in the world with that email address (isn't that nice?). So if anyone, anywhere in the world, sends a message to that address, it reaches you and you alone.

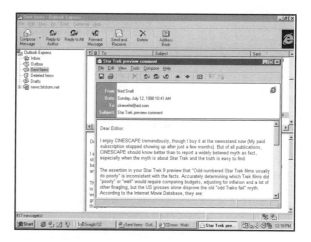

Have a Discussion

You learn how to use email, mailing lists, and news-groups in Parts 5, "Finding Other Stuff," and 6, "Exchanging Email."

Using your email client program, you can join mailing lists related to topics that interest you. Members of a mailing list automatically receive news and other information—in the form of email messages—related to the list's topic. Often, members can send their own news and comments to the list, and those messages are passed on to all members.

The Internet's principal discussion venue is the newsgroup, a sort of public bulletin board. Thousands of newsgroups exist, each centering on a particular topic—everything from music to politics, and from addiction recovery to TV shows. Newsgroup messages are stored on news servers; to read the messages and post your own messages, you need a client called a newsreader.

Chat

Exchanging messages through email and newsgroups is great, but it's not very interactive. You type a message, send it, and wait minutes, hours, or days for a reply. Sometimes, you want to communicate in a more immediate, interactive, "live" way. That's where Internet Relay Chat—a.k.a. "IRC" or just "Chat"—comes in.

Although it can be fun, Chat is also the riskiest place on the Internet; see Chapters 30, 31, and 32.

Using chat client programs, folks from all over the world contact Chat servers and join one another in live discussions. Each discussion takes place in a separate chat "room" or "channel" reserved for discussion of a particular topic. The discussion is carried out through a series of typed messages; each participant types his or her contributions, and anything anyone in the room types shows up on the screens of everyone in the room.

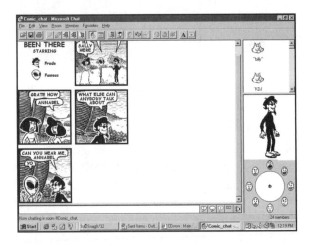

Have a Voice/Video Conference

With voice/videoconferencing, you converse long-distance without long-distance charges.

In addition to Chat, there are other ways to have a live conversation over the Internet. For example, you can hold voice and video conferences through the Internet, wherein you can see and hear your partners, and they can see and hear you. Your conversation partner can be anywhere in the world. This enables you, in effect, to have a long-distance phone call (even an international one) with no long-distance charges! (See Chapter 28, "Getting Started with Voice and Video Conferencing.")

Cheat Sheet

Using the Internet Without Buying a Computer

Instead of buying a computer and subscribing to an Internet service, you may be able to use computers and Internet accounts (within limits) supplied by

- Your school or the company you work for
- Your local public library
- A *cyber café*, a coffee house with Internet terminals for use by its patrons

What About WebTV?

WebTV is an Internet terminal that attaches to your TV set. It's cheaper than buying a computer for the Net, but also not nearly as powerful or versatile.

Getting the Speed You Need

Modems come in various speeds, from 9,600bps (9.6k) to 56k. A 33.6k or 56k modem is best for Web surfing.

Choosing a 56k Modem

If you are buying a 56k modem, choose one that supports the new V.90 standard.

Choosing a Computer

Web surfing demands a powerful computer with a fast, 32-bit processor and plenty of memory.

- On a PC, look for a Pentium processor (200MHz or faster) and at least 24–32MB of RAM.
- On a Mac, look for a 68040 or PowerPC processor and at least 24–32MB of RAM.
- On either type of computer, get a sound card, speakers, and microphone, and as large a hard disk as you can afford.

What Hardware Do You Need?

2

Do you have a computer made within the last 10 years? Then odds are you can get it onto the Internet. The power of your hardware doesn't have that much to do with whether you can get *on* the Net. But it has everything to do with what you can *do* there.

Basic Survival

Using the Internet Without Buying a Computer

The overwhelming majority of folks just getting online now are doing so through their own personal Mac or PC, at home or at work. That's the main scenario, and that's where much of this book's focus will rest.

However, many folks online are not using PCs or Macs, or even using their own computers, or signing up with an Internet provider, and are opting instead for the alternatives described in the following list. These methods are also a great way to get a taste of the Net while you're still trying to make up your mind about the Internet or saving up for that new computer.

These options entail compromises that make them poor long-term substitutes for a computer and Internet account.

- **School or Company Computer.** If the company you work for or school you attend has an Internet account, you may be permitted to use the organization's computers to explore the Net (usually within strict guidelines). Locate and speak to a person called the network administrator or system administrator; he or she holds the keys to the computer system, and is responsible for telling you whether you may use the system.

- **Public Library.** Many public libraries have Internet terminals set up for use by patrons. You may use these terminals to do quick research on the Web or newsgroups. You cannot use them for email, and library machines are never equipped for chat. Even if they were, it's not polite to hog a library PC (as a few evil people do) for a long, chatty Internet session.

You could probably afford your own computer with what you'll spend at a cyber cafe on Hawaiian Mocha and scones.

• **Cyber Café.** In all cool cities, you can find *cyber cafés*, coffeehouses equipped with Internet-connected computers so patrons can hang out, eat, drink, and surf. Some cyber cafés let you have an email address (for a fee), so you can send and receive email.

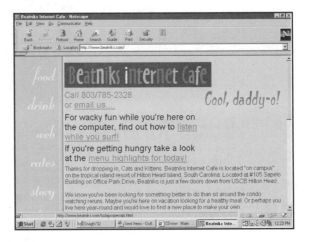

What About WebTV?

WebTV is a relatively new product based on the premise that there are people who want to use the Internet but don't want a computer. Instead of buying a PC or Mac, all you need for WebTV is a WebTV terminal (a small box that sits on or near your TV) and a subscription to the WebTV Internet service.

The WebTV terminal uses your TV as a display, and you navigate the Internet through the terminal's wireless remote control and/or an optional wireless keyboard. It uses your telephone line to connect to the Internet, just like a computer does.

You can find WebTV terminals at electronics and appliance stores— anywhere that sells TVs and VCRs.

The WebTV scenario has a few advantages: First and foremost, it's cheap (less than $300 for the terminal, versus $1,200 and up for a decent PC or Mac).

WebTV is also comparatively easy to set up and use, if you use the WebTV Network Internet service, which is priced comparably with most other Internet providers. You can also use a WebTV terminal with almost any Internet provider; however, setup is more difficult and you lose a number of special WebTV features (unless you pay an extra $9.95 for access to the WebTV Network through your other Internet provider).

WebTV can't do some Internet activities, such as chat or getting software.

WebTV also has drawbacks. The investment you make in a full computer buys you not only an Internet machine, but also one you can use to write letters, pay bills, do your taxes, play games, listen to CDs, teach your kids Spanish, and much more. A WebTV terminal is a single-purpose machine: You can use it for the Internet, and nothing else.

Beyond Survival

About Modems

Odds are that you will use an ordinary modem and telephone line for your Internet connection, so you must consider the capabilities of your modem in choosing or upgrading your computer for Internet access.

15

A modem is a device that enables two computers to communicate with one another through phone lines. Using a modem, you can communicate through your regular home or business phone lines with the modem at your Internet provider.

It doesn't really matter what brand of modem you buy, or whether it's an internal modem (plugged inside your computer's case), an external one (outside the computer, connected to it by a cable), or even one on a PCMCIA card inserted in a notebook PC. What matters is the modem's speed.

Getting the Speed You Need

Modem speed is usually expressed in bits per second (bps) or kilobits per second (Kbps, sometimes shortened to just k).

The higher the number of Kbps, the faster the modem. The faster your modem is, the more quickly Web pages appear on your screen, which makes Web surfing more fun and productive.

A kilobit = 1,000 bits, so a 28.8k modem = a 28,800bps modem.

Modems for use with regular telephone lines are usually rated at one of the following speeds:

- 9,600bps (9.6k)
- 14,400bps (14.4k)
- 28,800bps (28.8k)
- 33,600bps (33.6k)
- 56,000bps (56k)

Faster modem

Even through a fast modem, some Web pages show up slowly because their Web server is slow or overworked.

The practical minimum modem speed for Internet cruising (including Web browsing) is 14.4k, although at that speed, you'll often face long, long waits for Web pages to appear. Today, you'll find the best balance of speed and affordability in 33.6k modems, which provide decent Internet performance at a reasonable price.

Note that modem speed is not the only thing that governs the speed with which things spring onto your screen. If it takes your computer a long time to process the information it receives, you'll see some delays that have nothing to do with modem speed. A fast computer is almost as important as a fast modem—it's a team effort.

Choosing a 56K Modem

Today, many folks are opting for the fastest modems that can be used through a regular phone line: 56k. Most new computers today come equipped with 56k modems, as well.

At this writing, a new standard has just emerged for 56k modems. Called V.90, it will soon be the standard used for all 56k Internet access. When purchasing a 56k modem, be sure it's V.90-compatible, or easy to upgrade to V.90.

During the transition to V.90, there are two other standards in use:

Many non-V.90 modems can be upgraded to V.90 just by downloading and running a program on the manufacturer's Web site.

- Kflex

- X2

Some Internet providers (see Chapter 4, "About Internet Accounts") support both standards, but some support only one or the other. So if you have a Kflex modem, for example, your Internet provider must support the Kflex standard to provide you with 56k access to the Internet.

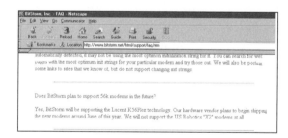

Choosing a Computer

Almost any computer—even an older one—can be used to get on the Internet. But to take full advantage of what the Internet offers, you need a fairly new, up-to-date model, if not the top of the line.

You see, some Internet tasks, such as email, demand little processing power from a computer and don't require a really fast Internet connection. However, the main thing most newcomers to the Net want is the Web, and browsing the Web is just about the most difficult task you can ask your computer to do.

Java—used in some Web pages for advanced features— requires a 32-bit chip such as a 486, Pentium, or Mac 68040.

To take full advantage of the Web, a computer must be able to display and play the multimedia content—graphics, animation, video, and sound—that's increasingly built in to Web pages. Such tasks require a fast processor and plenty of memory.

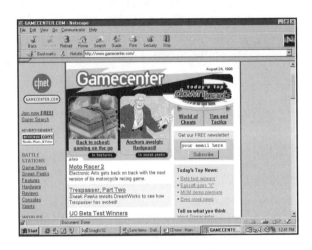

A PC for the Internet

A 486 PC may struggle with Java, online video, and other heavily-dirty Net stuff.

To make the most of today's Internet, the minimum reasonable PC would be equipped as follows:

- Processor. A Pentium processor (or its cloned equivalent) is recommended for its capability to support the pre-ferred operating systems listed next; look for a Pentium rated at 200MHz or faster. A 486 D×2 or 486 D×4 processor makes a workable, budget-minded alternative, provided that the PC also contains sufficient memory.

- Operating System. Windows 95, Windows 98, and Windows NT are all good choices. Windows 98 may be the best choice for many, because it features a built-in Web browser and an easy-to-use program for setting up your Internet connection.

- Monitor. The ideal display for Web browsing is config-ured to run at 800×600 resolution and 256 colors or greater. A resolution of 640×480 is an acceptable alterna-tive to 800×600, although a growing number of Web pages are designed to look their best when displayed at

800×600. Resolutions higher than 800×600 are not recommended, because they tend to make some items in Web pages appear too small.

- Memory. The bare minimum RAM for supporting Windows 95 and either of the leading Web browsers is 16MB. (Internet Explorer will run in 8MB on Windows 95, but not in its full installation, and not well.) But a more reasonable minimum memory for comfortable Internet cruising on Windows 95 is 24MB; for Windows 98 or NT, it's 32MB.

- Hard Disk. I can't tell you how big your hard disk should be, because I don't know how much other software you have. I can tell you that, after you've set up all your Internet software, your hard disk should be at least 25% empty. Windows Web browsers need a lot of free disk space for temporary data storage; when they don't have enough, performance and reliability suffer.

For installing software, the speed of the CD-ROM drive is unimportant; any drive will do.

- CD-ROM Drive. A CD-ROM drive is not required for any Internet activity. However, you may need one to install the Internet software you need to get started, if you acquire that software on CD.

- Other Peripherals. Plenty of fun sound and music is online these days, and to hear it you'll need a sound card and speakers (or headphones). If you want to make a long-distance phone call through the Internet or have a voice conference (see Part 8, "Live Communication"), connect a microphone to your sound card (or use your PC's built-in mic, if it has one), and for videoconferencing, add a PC video camera.

A Mac for the Internet

To make the most of today's Internet, the minimum reasonable Macintosh system would be equipped as follows:

- Processor. A 68040- or PowerPC-based Mac or Mac clone is recommended. A 68030-based system is a budget alternative, but cannot support the Mac OS8 operating system and may struggle with Java processing.

- Operating System. System 7 or OS8. If your Mac supports it, I strongly recommend OS8, which has a built-in, easy-to-use routine for setting up your Internet connection, built-in Java processing, and a complete set of Internet client programs.

- Display. The ideal display for Web browsing is configured to run at 800×600 resolution and 256 colors or greater. A resolution of 640×480 is an acceptable alternative to 800×600, although a growing number of Web pages are designed to look their best when displayed at 800×600. Resolutions higher than 800×600 are not recommended, because they tend to make some items in Web pages appear too small.

- Memory. Consider 16MB the workable minimum for Web browsing on any Mac. If you use OS8, 16MB will do, but 24MB is recommended.

- Hard Disk. Large enough to leave 25% free space after you have installed all of your software.

For installing software, the speed of the CD-ROM drive is unimportant; any drive will do.

- CD-ROM Drive. A CD-ROM drive is not required for any Internet activity. However, you may need one to install the Internet software you need to get started, if you acquire that software on CD.

- Other Peripherals. If you want to make a long-distance phone call through the Internet or have a voice conference (see Part 8), you'll need a microphone in your Mac, and for videoconferencing, you'll need a Mac-compatible video camera.

Cheat Sheet

What Do You Need?

Your Internet computer needs Internet communications software, plus a client program for each Internet activity you want to use (a browser for the Web, an email program, and so on). Which of these you need to get depends on which ones your computer came with.

Where Can You Get the Software?

To get the software you don't have—or replace the software you don't like—you can purchase commercial Internet software at a software store, or by phone/mail order. After you have at least the programs you need to get online, you can download new Internet software from the Web anytime you discover software you want.

Getting a Suite

To get all the client software you need in one fell swoop, get Netscape Communicator or Internet Explorer (version 4 or 5). Each includes a great Web browser plus email, newsgroup, and other clients.

What Software Do You Need?

Odds are that if you bought your computer recently, it already has all the software you need for Internet access, at least enough to get you started. Here's a rundown on what you need—or already have.

Basic Survival

What Do You Need?

To figure out what Internet software you need to get started, you must begin by looking at what your computer already has. Any computer for the Internet needs two types of software:

- Communications software. Establishes the connection between your computer and your Internet provider.

- Client software. Necessary for each activity you want to perform through the Net: a Web browser, an email client, a newsreader, and so on.

Here's the Internet software that comes automatically (and also the stuff that's left out) on popular computers:

Required Internet Software Each System Features and Lacks

Computer Type	Operating System	Internet Software Included	You Still Need
PC	Windows 98	Communications software, plus clients for Web browsing, email, newsgroups, and more.	None.

continues

Continued

Computer Type	Operating System	Internet Software Included	You Still Need
PC	Windows 95	Communications software. (A few clients are included, such as email, Telnet, and FTP. But these are not designed as beginner's clients, and no Web browser is included.)	Client software.
	Windows 3.1	None.	Communications software (such as Trumpet Winsock, supplied by most Internet providers to Windows 3.1 customers) and client software.
Mac	OS8	Communications software, plus clients for Web browsing, email, newsgroups, and more.	None.
	OS7 (System 7)	Communications software.	Client software.

Where Can You Get the Software?

The best place to get your start-up Internet software is from your Internet provider (which you learn more about in the next two chapters).

Why? Well, after you're online, you can easily acquire any software you want by downloading it (copying it from the Internet to your computer). All you need from your startup software is a way to begin.

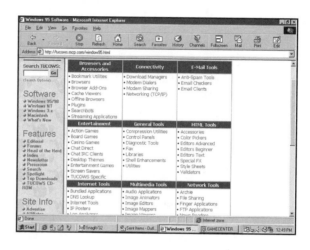

Appendix B, "Popular Internet Software and Where to Get It," shows Web addresses from which you can download popular Internet programs.

The software package your Internet provider supplies is usually given free of charge, and may include an easy-to-use setup routine, specially designed for your Internet provider, that makes setting up your connection easier.

As an alternative to using the software your provider supplies, you can walk into a software store and buy commercial Internet software right off the shelf. Most prepackaged Internet software is inexpensive ($5 to $50) and often comes with setup programs to conveniently sign you up for one or more Internet providers.

Beyond Survival

Getting a Suite: Internet Explorer or Netscape Communicator

Not long ago, the two major suppliers of Web browsing software—Microsoft and Netscape—recognized that it's confusing for Internet users to have to go out and pick separate client software programs for each Internet activity.

So both companies have developed "Internet suites"—bundles that include a whole family of Internet clients that install together and work together well.

Both suites include a Web browser, email client, newsgroup client, and voice/video conferencing software. Both also include a Web authoring tool for creating your own Web pages (see Part 10, "Your Very Own Web Page"). To all of that, Microsoft's suite adds a chat program.

You can buy either suite on CD at any software store, or order the CD direct from the developer. You may also be able to get a copy from your Internet provider.

About Netscape Communicator

The Communicator suite, sometimes called Netscape 4 or Navigator 4, is available for Windows 95/98/NT, Mac System 7/OS8, many UNIX versions, and Windows 3.1/Windows for Workgroups.

Unfortunately, Communicator for Windows 3.1/Windows for Workgroups requires a PC with the same power you need for Windows 95.

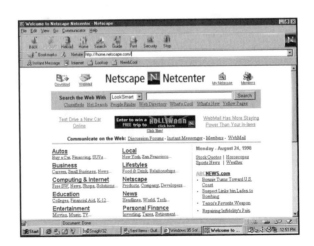

Both of the two major Internet client suites are available on CD-ROM at any software store.

After you're online, you can download the latest version of either suite from its maker's Web site.

The phone number for information or ordering Communicator is 650-937-3777.

The Communicator suite includes

- **Navigator.** The latest version of the most popular Web browser, Navigator combines an easy-to-use Web browsing interface with state-of-the-art support for advanced Web features, such as all multimedia types, frames, Java, enhanced security, and more.

- **Messenger.** Full-featured Internet email, including an address book (which makes recalling and using email addresses easier), support for messages containing multimedia, and tools for organizing messages.

- **Collabra.** An easy-to-use newsreader program that also enables you to create your own, private newsgroups.

- **Conference.** Voice/video conferencing software that enables you to have a live conversation with anyone else on the Internet who also uses Netscape Conference.

- **Page Composer.** A Web page editing environment that enables you to create and publish your own Web pages, almost as easily as creating a word processing document.

About Microsoft Internet Explorer 4

Unfortunately, IE4 for Windows 3.1/Windows for Workgroups requires a PC with the same power you need for Windows 95.

Internet Explorer 4, sometimes called IE4, is built in to Windows 98, and also available for Windows 95/NT, Mac OS7/OS8, UNIX, and Windows 3.1/Windows for Workgroups.

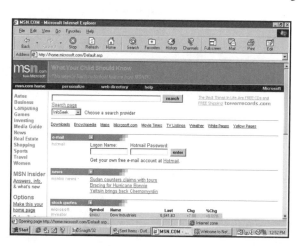

The phone number for information or ordering Internet Explorer is 800-485-2048.

The Internet Explorer suite includes

- **Internet Explorer Browser.** The latest version of the number two browser (close second to Navigator, and gaining), this browser features an easy-to-use Web browsing interface with state-of-the-art support for advanced Web features.

Don't confuse
Outlook
Express with
Microsoft
Outlook, a
more power-
ful program
that handles
email, schedul-
ing, and more.

NetMeeting,
FrontPage
Express, and
Chat are
included only in
the Windows
95/98/NT
versions of
IE4.

- **Outlook Express.** Many of the activities you perform in email and newsgroups are the same; in both, you compose, send, read, and organize messages. So Microsoft has combined email and newsreading into one client program, Outlook Express.

- **NetMeeting.** Voice/video conferencing software that enables you to have a live conversation with anyone else on the Internet who also uses NetMeeting.

- **FrontPage Express.** A Web page editing environment that enables you to create and publish your own Web pages, almost as easily as creating a word processing document.

- **Chat.** A unique chat client that presents the chat session on your screen in comic-strip form, turning each participant into a different cartoon character and displaying each character's words in a comic style "word balloon." (See Chapters 30, "Understanding Internet Relay Chat," 31, "Joining a Chat," and 32, "Contributing to a Chat.")

Cheat Sheet

What's an Internet Account?

An Internet account is a subscription with a company that provides you with access to the Internet, through your phone line and the company's own Internet connection. With your account, you get your own Internet username, password, and email address.

Special-Purpose Accounts

Popular "dial-up IP" accounts let you do anything online, and use any client software you want. Budget shell- and email-only accounts are cheaper, but limit your online activities and software options.

Knowing Your Internet Provider Options

You can get your Internet account from any of three main sources:

- A national Internet service provider (ISP), which supplies local Internet access to customers all over the United States or North America.
- A local ISP, one that provides access only to customers in the same city, town, or region. Local ISPs provide the same services as national companies, but often at a lower price.
- A commercial online service, such as America Online or CompuServe. Online services provide Internet service, plus other content and services solely for their customers, that is inaccessible by other Internet users. Online services are often the most expensive option, and sometimes provide mediocre Internet performance.

4

About Internet Accounts

To use the Net through a phone line at your home or office, you need to get an Internet account with an online service or Internet service provider. In this chapter, you learn what these accounts are all about and where to get them; in Chapter 5, "Choosing an Internet Provider or Online Service," you get tips on choosing the right company to sign up with.

Basic Survival

What's an Internet Account?

When you sign up with—*subscribe to*—an Internet service, you get what's called an *Internet account*.

With an Internet account, you get the right to use the Internet through the provider's lines, your own email address (so you can send and receive email), and all the other information you need to set up your computer for accessing the Internet through the service. From most providers, you may also get any communications or client software you need (refer to Chapter 3, "What Software Do You Need?").

About Dial-Up Accounts

The typical Internet account for an individual is called a "dial-up" account because you use it by "dialing up" the Internet provider through your modem and telephone line. These are sometimes also described as "IP" accounts. Dial-up IP accounts are the principal, general-purpose accounts offered by most Internet providers.

Besides dial-up accounts, there are other kinds, such as 24-hour "direct" connections (too costly for individuals).

Dial-up IP accounts support the use of all the popular client programs: Internet Explorer, Netscape Navigator, and so on. With a dial-up IP account, you have access to the full range of Internet activities and can use any client programs you want to.

Special-Purpose Accounts

Dial-up IP accounts are the norm now, and most of this book focuses on how you can use the Internet through such an account. There are other kinds of accounts that you may find valuable, however. "Shell" accounts and "email-only" accounts are also offered by many Internet providers as low-cost alternatives to dial-up IP accounts.

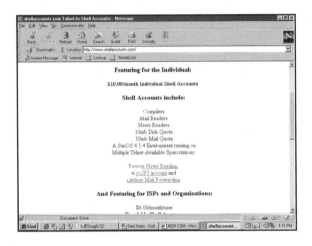

Shell accounts are cheaper than IP accounts, often available for $10 or less per month.

Shell account users typically use special client software that enables them to browse all the text on the Web (and use email and newsgroups) but not use most of the Web's multimedia, Java programs, or other cooler stuff. Those concessions enable you to use the Internet with a less powerful computer and slower modem than a dial-up IP account demands—you could use the Net effectively with a ten-year-old PC or Mac and a 2,400bps (2.4k) modem. But you can't use any of the popular Web browsers or experience all that the Web offers through a shell account.

Email-only accounts are available for free from some companies in exchange for the right to send you advertisements.

With an email-only account, you get full access to Internet email, and nothing else—no Web, no newsgroups, no chat, no shoes, no shirt, no service. You have access to mailing lists, however (see Chapter 24, "Subscribing to a Mailing List"), which enable you to get much of what you see in newsgroups via email. Email accounts can be run from the lowliest of computers, and usually cost around $2 to $5 per month.

Beyond Survival

Knowing Your Internet Provider Options

You can get your Internet account from any of three main sources:

- A national Internet service provider (ISP)
- A local ISP that is headquartered in your city or town
- A commercial online service, such as America Online

About the Commercial Online Services

Make sure your choice offers a dial-up number for connecting that is a local phone call from your computer.

With some online services and ISPs, you get a cheaper rate if you pay a year up front rather than monthly.

You've no doubt heard of at least one of the major online services, such as America Online (AOL) or CompuServe (CSi). These services promote themselves as Internet providers, and they are—but with a difference.

In addition to Internet access, these services also offer unique activities and content not accessible to the rest of the Internet community. These services have their own chat rooms, newsgroup-like message boards (often called "forums"), online stores, and reference sources that only subscribers to the service can use.

Setting up for online services is easy: Install the free software, start it up, and follow the onscreen instructions.

Online services used to be dramatically more expensive than ISPs. But lately, they've adopted pricing policies that are generally competitive with the local and national ISPs, although you can still usually get a better deal from a regular ISP than from any online service. The three main online services are

- America Online (AOL)—(800-827-6364) America Online is the most popular of the online services, largely because of aggressive marketing and initial ease-of-use. The non-Internet content is indeed the easiest to use of all services. The Internet access, however, is notoriously slow, and busy signals continue to be a problem.

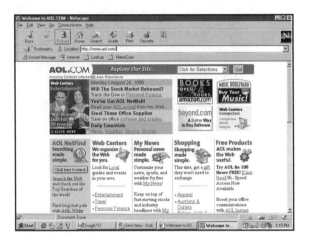

- CompuServe (CSi)—(800-848-8199) CompuServe wasn't the first online service, but it's the oldest still in operation, and it was once the undisputed king. That legacy leaves CompuServe with an unbeatable range of local access numbers.

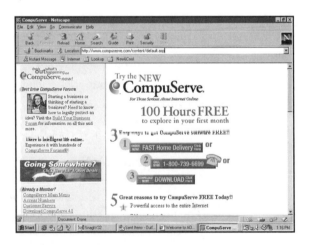

Signup software for MSN is built in to Windows 95 and Windows 98. To sign up, double-click the MSN icon.

- The Microsoft Network (MSN)—(800-FREE-MSN) The Microsoft Network started out in 1995 as a service much like AOL. It has since evolved away from the online service model, to the point where it is now less an online service and more a national (actually international) ISP, although it still supplies some content accessible only to its subscribers.

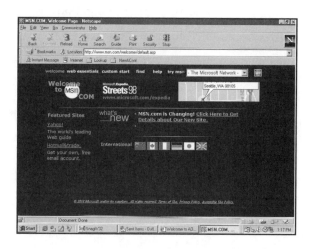

About Internet Service Providers (ISPs)

If you now have access to the Net through work, school, or a cyber cafe the table shows the Web address where you can learn more about each service.

Unlike an online service, an Internet service provider, or *ISP*, does not offer its subscribers special content that's not accessible to the rest of the Net. You get Internet access, period.

ISPs offer greater flexibility than online services, providing dial-up IP, shell, and email accounts, and enabling you (through dial-up IP accounts) to use virtually any client software you want to. ISPs also may offer more attractive rates and better service than the online services, although that's not always the case.

Large, national ISPs provide local access numbers all over North America.

A More-or-Less Random Selection of National ISPs

Company	Voice Number	Web Page Address
Earthlink	800-395-8425	www.earthlink.net
MindSpring	800-719-4664	www.mindspring.com

continues

35

Continued

Company	Voice Number	Web Page Address
Netcom	800-638-2661	www.ix.netcom.com
GTE Internet	800-927-3000	www.gte.com
Sprint	800-747-9428	www.sprint.com
MCI Internet	800-550-0927	www.mci.com
Micro-Net	800-480-9925	www.micronet.com
AT&T WorldNet	800-967-5363	www.att.net
PSINet	800-827-7482	www.psi.net
Voyager Online	800-864-0442	www.vol.com

When calling, always ask whether the ISP has a local access number in your area.

Finding a Local ISP

Besides the national ISPs, there are thousands of local ISPs in cities and towns everywhere. Typically, a local ISP cannot offer access numbers beyond a small, local service area of a few cities, towns, or counties. But it can provide reliable Internet access, personal service, and often the best rates you can get.

Finding a local ISP is getting easier all the time. Friends, coworkers, and local computer newsletters are all good sources for finding a local ISP. The folks at your nearest computer store or Radio Shack may also know of a good local ISP or two.

In your local Yellow Pages, look for ISPs under Internet, and then try Computers—Internet Services.

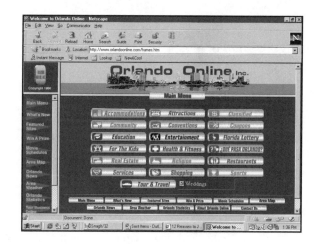

Cheat Sheet

Listening to Word of Mouth

Ask your friends which Internet provider they use, and if they're happy.

Comparing Plans and Rates

Choose an unlimited access, or "flat rate," plan to pay a fixed monthly fee ($15–$20) for unlimited use, or a "pay as you go" plan to pay by the minute.

Exploring the Billing Options

Services bill by credit card, mail, email, or telephone bill; choose the option that's best for you.

Checking Out Access Numbers

Make sure the provider you choose offers numbers for dialing into the Internet that are a local call (no long-distance toll) from each location where you may use the Net.

Considering Modem Speeds

Make sure your choice supports the fastest speed of your modem. If you have a 56k modem, make sure the provider supports your modem's 56k standard (X2, Kflex, or V.90).

What Software Is Included?

Look for a provider who supplies you with a good, free suite of client programs.

Do You Need Web Server Space?

If you want your own Web page, look for a provider who supplies free Web server space to its customers.

Are All Newsgroups Included?

Some providers don't carry every newsgroup. If you want access to all newsgroups, look for a provider who claims to carry them.

5

Choosing an Internet Provider or Online Service

Now that you know about the kinds of companies that can supply you with an Internet account, it's time to consider a few tips for choosing the best provider for you.

Basic Survival

Listening to Word of Mouth

Obviously, if you have friends who use the Internet, find out which services they use, and ask whether they're happy.

It's always a good idea to visit your friend and try out his or her Internet account to test the service they are recommending and to explore your other options.

Always find out if a local ISP has a local number for you; even if your friend lives within the service area, you may not.

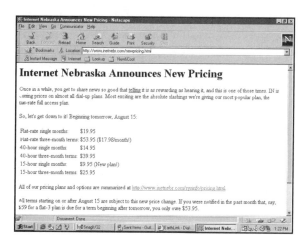

Comparing Plans and Rates

Most providers offer a range of different pricing plans, just to confuse you. (It's like choosing a long-distance phone plan—do you go with the plan that's a dime at night and a quarter during the day, or the one that's fifteen cents all the time, or the one that's 20% off after $20 and free on Tuesdays? Cripes.)

Sometimes, you get a cheaper rate if you pay a year's monthly charges in advance.

Some ISPs charge a "startup fee" on top of the first month's charges. Better providers don't.

Most people end up spending many more hours online than they think they will at first.

The kinds of plans you'll see most often, however, are Unlimited Access (or "flat rate") and Pay as You Go:

> Unlimited Access, or "Flat Rate" Plans—For a monthly fee of between $15 and $25, you can use the Internet all you want. In the last few years, such accounts have become the norm, and are available from virtually all online services and ISPs. Flat rate plans free you from having to think about how much time you're spending online.

> Except for folks who expect to use the Internet only sparingly, flat rate plans make the most sense. While exploring the Net, you don't want to feel like you must keep one eye on the clock.

> Pay as You Go or "Per Hour" Plans—These plans charge you according to the number of minutes per month you actually use the service. They typically start out with a monthly minimum charge (around $5–$10) and a number of "free" hours you can use the service (usually from 5 to 20 hours).

> In any month where you don't exceed the number of "free" hours, you pay only the monthly minimum. But in any month where you exceed the free hours, you pay the minimum plus an extra $1–$2 or more per hour for each hour over the limit.

> To decide whether you should go with such a plan, you must guess the number of hours you expect to use the Internet each month, calculate the cost under Pay as You Go, and compare that to the provider's flat rate plan.

Look for an ISP that lets you switch between plan types for free, so you can adapt if your first choice doesn't match your needs.

Exploring the Billing Options

Most providers bill your monthly charges automatically to any major credit card. Some local ISPs can bill you by mail, and some others can actually add your monthly Internet charges to your regular monthly telephone bill.

All other things being equal, lean toward the provider who will bill you in the way that's most convenient for you.

Checking Out Access Numbers

First, you want a provider that offers a local access number—a number for dialing into the service that is not a toll call—in the area where you use your computer (presumably your home or office). But you may need more than one local access number. What if...

Some local phone companies also offer Internet access, but not necessarily to every area they serve.

Just because a provider serves your area code doesn't mean it has an access number that's a local call from your exchange.

• You intend to use your account from both home and work, using two different computers or bringing a notebook computer back and forth. Does the provider offer a local access number for each location?

• You want to be able to use the Internet when you travel. Does the provider offer local access everywhere you and your computer might go?

If you really want access from everywhere (even when you travel), you're probably going to wind up with one of the online services or larger national ISPs who offer the greatest number and range of local access numbers. For a home/work setup, you'll need a national provider or a local ISP whose service area includes both your home and your job location.

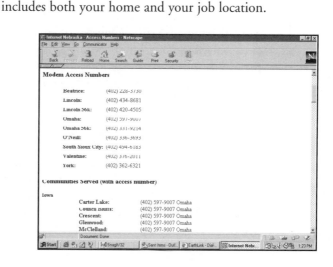

Beyond Survival

Considering Modem Speeds

Make sure the provider you select supports the maximum speed of your modem. If you use a 56k modem to access an Internet provider who supports only 33.6k (and slower) modems, you'll use the Internet at 33.6k, and your costly, speedy modem gains you nothing.

When your modem speed and your provider's modem speed differ, the connection runs at the speed of the slower modem.

Many providers support 56k modems now, although a few may charge extra for such fast access. Keep in mind that 56k access demands a clean, clear phone connection. Even if your provider offers 56k access and you use a 56k modem, you'll probably notice that your Internet connection often runs at a slower speed to compensate for line noise.

Finally, if you want 56k access to the Net, make sure the ISP you choose supports 56k access for the standard your modem uses (V.90, X2, or Kflex; refer to Chapter 2, "What Hardware Do You Need?")

What Software Is Included?

The online services usually require that you use a software package they supply, for setting up your connection, using their non-Internet content, and often for using the Internet, too.

That software may be included on the signup CD (the one you find bundled with magazines, sent in junk mail, or stuck in your cereal box, which you can also get by calling the service), or some of it might be transferred to your computer automatically during signup.

If your ISP gives you outdated programs, use them to get up and running, then download the new stuff from the Web.

Most ISPs can also supply you with any communications or client software you require, although using the ISP's software package is usually optional. If you need software to get started (refer to Chapter 3, "What Software Do You Need?"), you may want to consider what each ISP offers as a software bundle. Most offer a version of Netscape or Internet Explorer (possibly not the newest version of either) free to all new subscribers.

Do You Need Web Server Space?

If you think you might want to publish your own Web pages (see Part 10, "Your Very Own Web Page"), you'll need space on a Web server to do so. Some ISPs offer a small amount of Web server space free to all customers; others charge an additional monthly fee.

Are All News- groups Included?

Remember, you can always quit and try another service if your first choice disappoints you.

You'll learn all about newsgroups in Chapter 26, "Getting Started with Newsgroups." For now, just be aware that there are tens of thousands of newsgroups (the total changes daily as new groups are added and old ones die), and that not all providers give you access to all of them.

Some providers—including, to varying extents, the online services—take it upon themselves to censor newsgroups, preventing their subscribers from accessing any that might contain strong sexual or other controversial content. If that censorship appeals to you, keep in mind that the approach generally blocks access not only to genuinely racy groups, but also to many perfectly benign, G-rated groups that get lumped together with the racy ones.

If you want easy, universal access to all newsgroups, be sure to choose an ISP that promises to supply it.

Cheat Sheet

Keys to Your Account: Username and Password

The three most important pieces of information you need from your
Internet provider to connect to the Internet are

- *Local Access Number.* The telephone number your modem dials to
  connect to your Internet provider.
- *Username.* Your unique name on the service you've chosen.
- *Password.* A secret word known only to you and your provider, to
  ensure that only you can use your account.

Using a Signup Program

The easiest way to set up your computer is to get a signup disk from the
Internet provider you've chosen; the disk contains a signup program that
automatically sets up your account with a little help from you. Just start
the program and do what it tells you to.

Setting Up Without a Signup Program

Alternatively, you can set up for any ISP (but not for an online service) by
running the Internet setup routines included with Internet Explorer and
Netscape Navigator. These programs prompt you for the communications
settings and other information your ISP tells you when you open your
account over the telephone; use that information to set up your communications software.

Connecting to the Internet

You've got your hardware and software, and you've selected a provider. It's time to get your computer connected to the Internet.

To connect to the Internet, the communications software on your computer has to be supplied with certain information about your Internet provider. You can give it this information by running the signup program that you received from your Internet provider or by configuring your communications software on your own.

Basic Survival

Keys to Your Account: Username and Password

"Username" is sometimes also called user name, user ID, or userID.

"Logging on" is sometimes also called "logging in" or "signing in."

No matter how you set up your account and computer, you'll wind up with three pieces of information that are essential to getting online:

- Local access number. The telephone number your modem dials to connect to your Internet provider's computer.

- Username. To prevent just anybody from using its service, your Internet provider requires each subscriber to use a unique name, called a username, to connect.

- Password. To prevent an unauthorized user from using another's username to sneak into the system, each subscriber must also have his or her own secret password.

Entering your username and password to go online is called "logging on."

If you use a signup program to set up your account and computer, you'll choose your username and password while running the program. If you set up your computer without a signup disk, you'll choose a username and password while on the

The Mac's OS8 system includes signup software for America Online. Double-click the AOL icon to sign up.

phone with your provider to open your account. (Both procedures are described later in this chapter.)

Every user of a particular Internet provider must have a different username. If you choose a large provider (such as AOL), there's a good chance that your first choice of username is already taken by another subscriber. In such cases, your provider instructs you to choose another username, or to append a number to the name to make it unique. For example, if the provider already has a user named CarmenDiaz, you can be CarmenDiaz2, or CarmenDiaz25.

Using a Signup Program

Most new PCs come with signup programs for AOL and other services; look for the icons on your desktop.

A special signup program is required for each online service, and many ISPs can also supply you with a signup program for your computer. I recommend using signup programs whenever they're available, even when they're optional. The program automatically takes care of all the communications configuration required in your computer, some of which can be tricky for inexperienced users.

You can get free signup disks by mail from the providers, just by calling them on the telephone (see Chapter 4, "About Internet Accounts"). Also, signup programs often come preinstalled on new computers and in computer magazines and junk mail.

Running a Typical Signup Program

Some ISPs can charge you via a debit card, or automatically deduct your fee from your bank account.

Before running a signup program, make sure your modem is connected to a telephone line because the signup software usually dials the provider at least once during the signup process. Also, make sure you have a major credit card handy; you'll need to enter its number and expiration date to set up payment.

You'll find instructions for starting the program on a page or card that accompanies it, or printed right on the CD or disk. After you start the program, just follow its lead. The program prompts you to type in your name, address, phone number, and payment information, and to choose a logon username and password, email address, and email password. The program may also present you with a list of payment plans from which to choose.

When you choose each of the following during signup, be sure to jot it down for later reference:

- Your username and password for logging on.

- Your email address.

- Your email password (may be different from your Internet password; used to retrieve email others have sent to you).

- The telephone number of your provider's customer service and technical support departments.

Once or twice during the signup process, the program uses your modem to contact the provider. It does this to verify your payment information, find the best local access number for you, check that your selected username is not already taken, and ultimately to send all of your information to the provider to open your account.

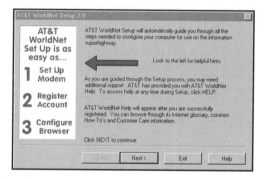

Beyond Survival

Setting Up Without a Signup Program

When you don't use a signup disk, you must set up your account with your selected Internet provider over the telephone first, and then configure your computer. While setting up your account, your provider tells you all the communications settings required for the service, and works with you to select your local access number, username, and password.

It's important that you make careful notes of everything your provider tells you. You'll use all that information when setting up. In addition to your access number, logon username, and password, you'll probably come out of the conversation with the following information:

Numbered addresses may be called IP or DNS addresses and look like 248.143.138.2

- One or more numbered addresses required for communicating with the provider. These will take the form of four groups of numbers separated by periods.

- The addresses of the provider's email and news servers. Email server addresses may be described as SMTP and POP3 servers (you usually need one of each), and news servers may be described as NNTP servers.

You don't need to understand these abbreviations; just know that NNTP is a news server and SMTP and POP3 are email servers.

- Your email address, the one others can use to send email to you.

- Your email password, required for retrieving email people have sent to you.

- The voice telephone number and hours of the provider's customer service or technical support departments.

- Any other special communications steps or settings the particular provider requires.

No matter how you go about it, setting up your computer for the Internet is a simple matter of entering this information in your communications software. After that's done, you can go online.

Setting Up Windows 95/98 for an ISP

You use this procedure only to set up for an ISP, not an online service.

Short of using a signup program, the next easiest way to set up an ISP account on a PC running Windows 95 is to install Internet Explorer or Netscape Communicator (see Chapter 3, "What Software Do You Need?").

Each of these software suites includes an easy-to-use program for configuring your Windows 95 Internet connection. These programs lead you through each step of the process, prompting you for all the required settings.

Windows 98
has Internet
Explorer
4—and its
automatic
setup
program—
built-in.

Using these programs is almost as easy as using a signup disk, except that they don't sign you up with your ISP—you must take care of that first—and they prompt you for addresses and other setup information, which a signup program can supply for itself.

To use the setup program—called Connection Wizard—that is bundled with Internet Explorer 4 (IE4), follow these steps (after each step, click the Next button):

You may see
small
differences
from these
steps, depend-
ing on your
IE4 version.
Just do
what the
wizard says.

1. Install IE4. (Skip this step if you have Windows 98.)

2. In Windows, click Start, then choose Programs, Internet Explorer, Connection Wizard.

3. Read the Welcome dialog box (if one appears).

4. In the Setup Options dialog box, choose the middle choice (either "I want to set up a new connection..." or "I have an existing account..." (whichever is offered in your version).

The top
choice on the
Setup Options
dialog box
opens a
referral
service to
choose an
ISP.

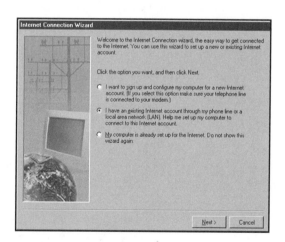

5. Choose Create a New Dial-Up Connection.

6. Complete the area code and phone number used to connect to your ISP. (Your communications software won't dial the area code if doing so is unnecessary; it just needs it to know that your ISP is a local call.)

49

7. Enter your Internet username and password.

8. On the Advanced Settings dialog box, choose one of the following options:

- If your ISP gave you no numbered addresses to enter, click No and move on to step 9.

- If your ISP supplied you with numbered addresses, click Yes. You'll proceed through a short series of dialog boxes that prompt for the addresses and other settings. When you arrive at the Dial-Up Connection Name dialog box, go to step 9.

9. Type a name (anything you like) to identify your Internet account. If you don't type anything, the wizard names the connection "Connection to" plus the telephone number.

10. In the Set Up Your Internet Mail Account dialog box, choose Yes.

11. Choose Create a New Internet Mail Account.

12. In the Your Name dialog box, type your full name.

13. In the Internet Email Address account box, type your complete email address, as given to you by your ISP.

14. In the Internet Mail Logon dialog box, type your email username and password.

15. In the Friendly Name dialog box, give your email account a name to identify it. Use any name you like.

When typing the password, **** appears instead of the password, so no one can peek over your shoulder to steal your password.

16. In the Set Up Your Internet News Account dialog box, choose Yes.

17. Choose Create a New Internet News Account.

18. In the Your Name dialog box, type your full name.

19. In the Internet News Email Address dialog box, enter your complete email address (if it does not already appear in the box).

20. In the Internet News Server Name dialog box, type the news server address.

21. In the Friendly Name dialog box, give your news account a name to identify it. Use any name you like.

22. In the Set Up Your Internet Directory Service dialog box, choose whether to set up an Internet Directory Service now or leave it for another Connection Wizard session.

Anytime you want to make changes to your Internet communications settings, just start over from step 2

Setting Up a Mac for an ISP

Just as in Windows 95, the easiest way to set up your Mac connection (short of an ISP signup program) is to install the Mac version of Internet Explorer or Netscape Communicator, and use the setup program each of these programs contains.

I can't show you the exact steps (they'll differ depending on what you get), but just follow the prompts, reading each prompt carefully, and you'll do fine. If you encounter terms you don't understand, look them up in this book's Glossary or Index.

The Mac's OS8 system includes signup software for America Online. Click the AOL icon to sign up.

PART 2

Browsing the Web

This may be your favorite part of this Cheat Sheet book.
Most folks who get online today do so for the enormous
wealth of fun and information they can find on the Web.
In this part, you join them, by

- Surfing Straight to a Web Site

- Navigating the Web

- Getting Back to Places You Like

- Protecting Your Privacy

Cheat Sheet

Getting Online

Locate the icon or menu item for your connection program (created when you set up your connection), open it, enter your username and password, and click Connect or OK.

(In some setups, the connection program may open automatically when you open your Web browser.)

Understanding Web Page Addresses

Web page addresses, known as URLs, are what you type in a Web browser to go directly to a particular Web site or page, and they look like this:

```
http://www.buick.com
```

All Web URLs begin with `http://` or `https://`, but you may leave off that part when typing a URL in a recent version (3 or later) of Internet Explorer or Netscape Navigator.

Entering URLs

To go to any page, find the address box in your browser—a text box, usually in the toolbar area—type the URL there, and then press Enter. Be careful to spell, punctuate, and capitalize the URL exactly as shown.

Changing Your Home Page

When you first open your Web browser, it goes immediately to a page configured as your startup, or "home," page. You can choose which page to use as your home page by changing the home page URL in a dialog box in your browser.

Surfing Straight to a Web Site

7

Here it is, the $64,000 hour. The Web is the main reason interest in the Internet has exploded in the last five years, and the main thing that draws newcomers to it. In this chapter, you pick up the basics of getting online and getting to a Web site. In Chapter 8, "Navigating the Web," you'll learn more about getting easily from place to place.

Basic Survival

Getting Online

After your account, connection, and client software are all set up on your computer (see Chapter 6, "Connecting to the Internet"), you can connect to the Internet at will by opening your connection program.

Exactly how you open your connection program differs, depending on your computer, the software you select, and whether you choose an ISP or an online service:

It usually doesn't matter whether you connect and then open your client, or open your client and then connect.

- Online services generally deposit an icon that looks like their logo on your Windows or Mac desktop. To go online, click that icon.

- If you used an ISP signup program, you will probably also see a new icon or easily identifiable menu item for connecting.

Often, online services deposit a new menu item in your Programs or Apple menu, too.

- If you configured your connection on your own, you start it by clicking the Dial-Up Networking icon you created in Windows 95 (open My Computer, then double-click the Dial-Up Networking folder), or the Config PPP icon in Mac System 7 (in the MacTCP control panel).

- If you used Internet Explorer's or Navigator's setup program, you may open your connection by opening the Internet Explorer or Netscape Navigator browser. Doing so automatically starts the connection software as well as the browser.

After the connection program opens, you're usually presented with a dialog box in which to type your Internet username and password. Type your username and password. Then click the button on the dialog box labeled OK, Connect, or Open.

When typing the password, **** appears instead of the password, so no one can peek over your shoulder to steal your password.

Your connection program instructs the modem to dial your Internet provider and sends your username and password to log you on.

If all goes well, you'll see a dialog box or message indicating that you are connected. That dialog box usually also is used for disconnecting when you're finished using the Net. Choose Close or Disconnect on the dialog box, or just close the dialog box, to go offline.

To disconnect in Windows 95/98, you may need to double-click the little connection icon in the far-right end of your taskbar

About Your "Home Page"

Most Web browsers are configured to go automatically to a particular Web page as soon as you open them and connect to the Internet. This page is generally referred to as the browser's "home page."

The page selected as your home page depends on your browser software and where you got it. For example,

- If you get Internet Explorer directly from Microsoft, it opens at a special "Start" page on Microsoft's Web server.

- If you get Netscape Navigator directly from Netscape, it opens automatically to a similar startup page at Netscape.

Home page is a.k.a. "startup" or "start" page.

However, if you get your software from your Internet provider, your browser is probably reconfigured with a new home page, one that's set up by your provider as a starting point for its subscribers. This home page also serves as a source of news and information about the provider and its services.

You don't have to do anything with your home page. You can just ignore it, and jump from it to anywhere on the Web you want to. But some home pages provide valuable resources, especially for newcomers.

Often, you'll find a great selection of links—text or pictures you can click to jump elsewhere (see Chapter 8)—on your home page to other fun or useful pages. If your home page happens to be one set up by your local ISP, the page may even contain local news, weather, and links to other pages with information about your community.

Understanding Web Page Addresses

If there's one thing about Web surfing that trips up newcomers, it's using Web page addresses effectively. So here and now, you'll get set straight on Web page addresses so you can leap online with confidence.

For the most part, you'll deal with only two kinds of addresses for most Internet activities:

- Email addresses, which are easy to spot because they always contain an "at" symbol (@); for example, clinton@whitehouse.com. You'll learn all about email addresses in Chapter 19, "Finding Phone Numbers and Email Addresses."

- Web page addresses, which never contain an @ symbol. Web page addresses are expressed as series of letters separated by periods (.) and sometimes forward slashes (/); for example: `www.microsoft.com/index/contents.htm`. (Web addresses often begin with "www," but not always.)

A Web page address is called a URL.

By typing a URL in your Web browser (as you learn to do shortly), you can go straight to that page, the page the URL "points to." Just to give you a taste of the possibilities, and to get you accustomed to the look and feel of a URL, here are the URLs of some fun and interesting Web sites.

A Few Out of the Millions of Fun and Interesting Web URLs

URL	Description
www.cnn.com	Cable News Network (CNN)
www.doonesbury.com	The Doonesbury comic strip
www.epicurious.com	A trove of recipes
www.scifi.com	The SciFi Channel
www.uncf.org	The United Negro College Fund
www.rockhall.com	Cleveland's Rock & Roll Hall of Fame museum
www.un.org	The United Nations
www.nyse.com	The New York Stock Exchange
college-solutions.com	A guide to choosing a college
www.sleepnet.com	Help for insomniacs
www.nasa.gov	The space agency's site

URL	Description
www.adn.com	The Anchorage, Alaska, Daily News
www.mommytimes.com	Parenting advice
us.imdb.com	The Internet Movie Database—everything about every film ever made
www.nhl.com	The National Hockey League

A URL is made up of several different parts. Each part is separated from those that follow it by a single, forward slash (/).

You can find more fun Web site URLs in Appendix A, "More Great Sites to Visit."

The first part of the URL—everything up to the first single slash (/)—is the address of a particular Web server. Everything following that first slash is a directory path and/or filename of a particular page on the server.

For example, consider the following fictitious URL:

The filename of the actual Web page is fudge.htm. (Web page files generally use a filename extension of .htm or .html.) That file is stored in a directory or folder called sundaes, which is itself stored in the icecream directory. These directories are stored on a Web server whose Internet address is www.dairyqueen.com.

Sometimes, a URL shows just a server address and no Web page filename. That's okay—many Web servers are set up to show a particular file to anyone who accesses the server (or a particular server directory) without specifying a Web page filename.

Do I Need the "http://" Part?

Technically, every Web page URL begins with `http://` or `https://`. But recent releases of Netscape Navigator and Internet Explorer no longer require you to type that first part. For example, using either of those browsers, you can surf to the URL

    http://www.mcp.com

just by typing

    www.mcp.com

Because of this change, Web page addresses often appear in advertising, books, and magazines with the `http://` part left off.

If you use a browser other than the Big Two (IE4 or Netscape) or use an older version of the Big Two, however, you probably have to include the `http://` part when typing URLs in your browser. For example, to go to `www.pepsi.com`, you must type

    http://www.pepsi.com

Finding the Address Box in Your Browser

Before you can jump to a page by entering its URL, you must find the place in your browser provided for typing URLs. The term used to describe this area varies from browser to browser, but to keep things simple, just call it the "address box."

Address box with URL
of current page

60

In both Internet Explorer and Netscape Navigator, you'll see the address box as a long text box somewhere in the toolbar area, showing the URL of the page you're currently viewing. If you don't see it, the toolbar that contains the address box might be switched off.

To switch on the toolbar that contains the address box:

- In Internet Explorer, choose View, Toolbars, and make sure a check mark appears next to Address Bar in the menu that appears. If not, click Address Bar. If you still don't see an address box, try dragging each toolbar to the bottom of the stack so that all toolbars are visible and none overlap.

- In Netscape Navigator, choose View, Show Location Toolbar. If you still don't see it, it's there, but collapsed so it's not visible. Click at the far-left end of each line in the toolbar area, and it should appear.

If you use a different browser, you may see an address box in the toolbar area, or at the bottom of the browser window. In some browsers, you may have to choose a menu item to display a dialog box that contains the address box. Look for a menu item with a name like "Enter URL" or "Jump to New Location."

Entering URLs

After you've found the address box, you can go to a particular address by typing the URL you want to visit in the box and pressing Enter. When the address box is in a toolbar, you usually must click in the address box first, then type the URL and press Enter. When typing URLs, keep the following in mind:

- Before you type, the URL of the current page already appears in the address box. In most browsers, if you click once in the address box, the whole URL there is highlighted, meaning that whatever you type next replaces that URL.

- If you click twice in the address box, the edit cursor appears there so you can edit the URL. That's a handy feature when you discover that you made a typo when first entering the URL.

If you're offline when you enter a URL, your connection program opens so you can connect and go where the URL leads.

61

URL Typing Tips

When typing the URL, be careful about the following:

- Spell and punctuate the URL exactly as shown, and do not use any spaces.

- Match the exact pattern of upper- and lowercase letters you see in the URL. Some Web servers are case-sensitive, and will not show you the page if you don't get the capitalization in the URL just right.

- Some URLs that don't end in .htm or .html end in a final slash (/), and some don't. But servers can be quirky about slashes. Always type a URL exactly as shown. But if that doesn't work, try adding or removing the final slash.

- If you do not use a recent version of Internet Explorer or Netscape Navigator, you probably must include the `http://` prefix at the beginning of the URL; for example, when you see a URL listed as `www.discover.com`, you must enter it in your address box as

```
http://www.discover.com
```

When you type a URL, your starting point doesn't matter—you can be at your home page, or on any other page.

Beyond Survival

Practicing Opening a Web Page

Honest, I'm not shilling for Macmillan Computer Publishing (MCP) here, even though MCP published this book. It's just that Web pages come and go. Most Web site URLs for large organizations work fine for years. But addresses can change, and Web pages and sites do disappear from time to time. I want to give you a reliable set of steps, and I have reasonable confidence that the MCP Web site will still be around when you read this.

To practice using a URL by connecting to the MCP Web site:

1. Connect to the Internet and open your Web browser.

2. Find your address box, and click in it once.

3. Type the URL

```
http://www.mcp.com
```

4. Press Enter. Macmillan's Web site appears.

If using a recent version of IE4 or Netscape, you can leave off the `http://` in step 3.

A slow-loading page doesn't mean a bad modem—some pages just appear slowly, especially if they have lots of pictures.

Changing Your Home Page

Your home page also appears if you click the Home button on your browser's toolbar.

On your Web travels, you'll discover many different pages you'll want to revisit. But you may also discover one page you like or need so much that you want to visit it first, every time you go online.

If you find such a page, why not make it your browser's home page, so your browser automatically goes straight to it every time you go online? Most browsers that use a home page—including Navigator and Internet Explorer—also enable you to choose that page.

To make any page your home page, all you have to do is find your browser's dialog box where the URL of the home page is selected, and replace that address with the address of the page you want to use as your new home page. You'll find that dialog box:

- In Internet Explorer 4, by choosing View, Internet Options, General.

- In Navigator 4, by choosing Edit, Preferences, and then choosing Navigator from the list that appears in the left side of the dialog box.

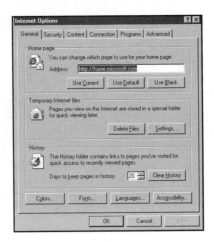

Both Internet Explorer and Navigator provide a way you can save the trouble of typing the URL when configuring a new home page.

In either browser, begin by browsing to the page you want to use as your home page. Next, open the dialog box on which you change the home page. Finally...

- In Navigator 4, click the Use Current Page button.

- In Internet Explorer 4, click the Use Current button.

Cheat Sheet

Finding and Using Links

Links can be represented in a page by:

- Text (usually underlined)
- Pictures
- Imagemaps (pictures in which clicking a different part of the picture activates a different link)

When you point to a link, the pointer changes to a pointing finger 👆. To use a link, point to it and click.

Using Navigation Buttons

Four buttons on your browser's toolbar are useful for jumping around the Web:

- **Back**   retraces your steps, taking you one step backward in your browsing each time you click it.
- **Forward**   reverses the action of Back.
- **Home**   takes you directly to your home page.
- **Stop**   immediately stops whatever the browser is doing.

Fussing with Frames

Some Web pages are split up into separate onscreen panes, called frames. Within each frame is a separate document, which you can scroll in its frame and use independently. To work in a frame, click there.

Understanding Multimedia

Multimedia files on the Web—sound, video, and so on— either play automatically when you open the page (inline multimedia) or play after you download them to your computer by clicking a link (external multimedia).

The capabilities of your browser determine which kinds of multimedia you can see and hear. You can expand a browser's multimedia capabilities with plug-ins and helpers (see Part 3, "Making Your Browser Do More").

8

Navigating the Web

Getting to a particular URL is only the start of most online excursions. Much of your online navigation will be done by clicking hyperlinks (usually called simply "links"), text, and pictures in a Web page that lead to other pages, files to download, and more. You'll also do an appreciable amount of Web navigation just by clicking buttons on your browser's toolbar, such as Back, Stop, and Home.

Basic Survival

Finding Links

You're not always going to find a link that takes you exactly where you want to go. URLs are like cars—they take you directly to a particular place. Links are like the bus—they often take you just to the right neighborhood.

It's not using links that can be tricky (all you do is point and click), it's finding them in Web pages that aren't designed well enough to make the links obvious. Links appear in a Web page in any of three ways:

Your browser usually controls the color in which text links are displayed.

- As text. You'll notice text in Web pages that appears to be formatted differently from the rest. The formatting differs depending on your browser, but link text is usually underlined and displayed in a different color (often purple or blue) than any other text in the page.

- As images. Any image you see in a Web page may be a link. For example, a company logo may be a link leading to a page containing information about that company.

- As imagemaps. An imagemap is a single image that contains not just one link, but several. Clicking different parts of the image activates different links.

Text Image
links links

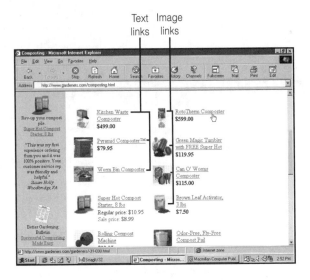

If you point to an object and the pointer does not change, that object isn't a link.

Text links are usually easy to spot because of their color and underlining. Image and imagemap links can be harder to spot at a glance.

But most browsers provide a simple way to determine what is and is not a link. Whenever the mouse pointer is on a link, it changes from the regular pointer to a special pointer that always indicates links—usually a hand with a pointing finger. Depending on your browser, when the finger appears you may also see the URL where that link leads displayed in the status bar, at the bottom of the browser window.

Pointer —

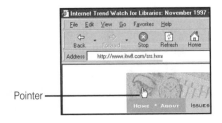

Using Navigation Buttons: Back, Forward, Home, Stop

These buttons look a little different in each browser.

In most browsers, you'll see a whole raft of toolbar buttons, many of which you'll discover as this book progresses. But by far, the most important are the Big Four: Back, Forward, Home, and Stop.

These buttons help you move easily back and forth among any pages you've already visited in the current online session, and to conveniently deal with the unexpected.

For example, when exploring a particular Web site, you often begin at a sort of "top" page that branches out to others. After branching out a few steps from the top to explore particular pages, you'll often want to work your way back to the top again, to start off in a new direction. The Big Four buttons make that kind of Web navigation simple, and typing-free.

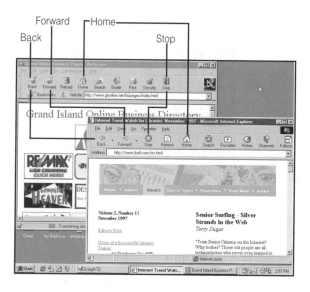

On the page you visited first in the current session, the Back button is disabled—there's nowhere to go back to.

Here's how you can use each of the Big Four buttons:

- Back ⬑ retraces your steps, taking you one step backward in your browsing each time you click it. For example, if you move from Page A to Page B, clicking the Back button takes you back to A. If you go from A to B to C, clicking Back twice returns you to A.

On the page
you visited last
in the current
session, the
Forward
button is
disabled—
there's
nowhere to go
forward to.

You can choose
your home
page; see
Chapter 7.

- Forward [icon] reverses the action of Back. If you've used Back to go backward from Page B to A, Forward takes you forward to B. If you click Back three times—going from D to C to B to A—clicking Forward three times takes you all the way ahead to D.

- Home [icon] takes you from anywhere on the Web directly to the page configured in your browser as "home" (see Chapter 7, "Surfing Straight to a Web Site"). Going Home is a great way to reorient yourself if you lose your way and need to get back to a reliable starting point.

- Stop [icon] immediately stops whatever the browser is doing. If you click Stop while a page is materializing on your screen, the browser stops getting the page from the server, leaves the half-finished page on your screen, and awaits your next instruction.

Back, Forward, and Home do not care how you got where you are. In other words, no matter what techniques you've used to browse through a series of pages—entering URLs, clicking links, using buttons, or any combination—Back takes you back through them, Forward undoes Back, and Home takes you home.

Practicing Using Links and Buttons

You can practice using links and buttons by following these steps:

1. Go to the MCP Web site at www.mcp.com.

2. Move the pointer around on the page, and notice where it turns into a pointing finger. That's where the links are.

3. Point to a link, and click it. You'll go somewhere. Where you go depends on which link you clicked.

4. Click Back. You return to the top MCP Web page.

5. Click another link.

6. On the page that appears, find and click yet another link.

7. Click Back twice. You return to the top MCP page.

8. Click Forward twice. You go ahead to where you just came back from.

In step 6, if
you see no
links, click
Back to
return to the
top MCP
page, and try
another route.

70

9. Try a new URL: Enter www.akc.org (the American Kennel Club).

10. From the AKC page, click Back once. You return to a page at MCP.

11. Click Home. Welcome Home.

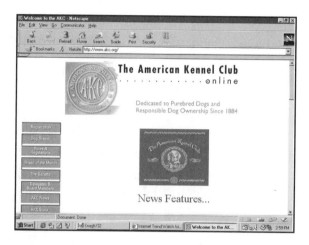

Beyond Survival

Fussing with Frames

Some pages you'll find are split up into *frames*, two or more separate panes. Some call such pages frames pages.

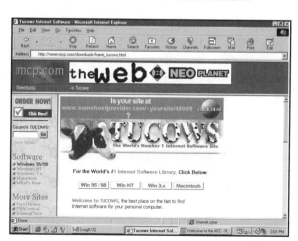

Internet Explorer and Navigator both support frames, but some other browsers do not.

In effect, each pane in a frames page contains its own, separate little Web page. That enables each pane to operate independently of the others; for example, clicking a link in one pane can change the contents of another.

Some folks get all boxed up by frames, but using a frames-based page isn't really that tricky. Just remember the following tips:

- To use the links or other stuff in a particular pane, click anywhere within the pane first to select that pane as the "active" pane. Then do what you want there. Anytime you move to another pane, click there before doing anything.

- Some panes have their own scrollbars. When you see scrollbars on a pane, use them to scroll more of the pane's contents into view.

- While you're on a frames page, the Back and Forward buttons take you back and forth among the panes you've used in the current frames page, not among pages. Sometimes, it can be tough to use Back to back out of a frames page to the page you saw before it; at such times, it's often easier to enter a new URL or click Home to break free of the frames, then go from there.

- Some pages use borderless frames, and so do not appear at first glance to be frames pages. But after a little experience, you'll quickly learn to identify any frames page when it appears, even when the frames are implemented subtly.

If your browser can't do frames, choose the no-frames version.

Because some people don't like frames—and because some older browsers can't display them—many frames pages are preceded by a non-frames top page that provides two links: One for displaying the frames page, and another for displaying the same content in a no-frames version.

Understanding Multimedia

Strictly speaking, multimedia describes everything on the Web that's not text, including any images that appear in Web pages. But images that are incorporated into the layout of a Web page aren't really part of the whole multimedia issue, because there's no trick to seeing them: Any graphical browser can show the images in a Web page automatically.

When I say multimedia, I'm talking about such advanced Web capabilities as playing video clips, sound clips, and animation. I'm also talking about hearing and seeing live audio and video broadcasts through the Web.

This multimedia comes in two basic types:

- Inline. Incorporated into the page so it plays or displays automatically when you go to the page.

- External. Stored in a separate file you open by clicking a link.

A 30-second video clip may take a half-hour or more to download.

As you'll learn the hard way, external multimedia files can be very large and may take a long time to travel to your computer before they play.

Playing Multimedia

For your part, playing multimedia on the Web requires only the skills you already possess—opening Web pages and clicking links. It's the browser that must know what to do with the multimedia files that you encounter while browsing.

Each type of online multimedia is a different kind of file, requiring a different program to play it. For example, there are at least a dozen different types of video and sound files, and each type requires a different program to play it. (There are some programs that play a variety of file types, however, such as Windows's built-in Media Player.)

IE4 and Communicator (see Chapter 3, "What Software Do You Need?") have native support for most popular multimedia types.

A browser supports this multimedia in any of three ways:

- Native support. The capability to handle certain types of multimedia is built in to the browser.

- Plug-in. A plug-in is an optional add-in to a browser that endows it with new capabilities, such as support for a multimedia type the browser does not support natively.

A plug-in creates the illusion of native support for the new features it adds to the browser.

- Helper. A helper is a program separate from the browser that handles a particular file type. When encountering a file type for which it has no native support or plug-in, a browser may open another program on your computer to handle the file. For example, some browsers lack native support for video files using the extension .AVI. However, Windows 95 has a built-in program, Media Player, that plays .AVI files. When a browser lacking native support for .AVI files hits an .AVI file, it automatically opens a helper, Media Player, to play the file.

You learn about using plug-ins and helpers in Part 3.

There is a long, complicated list of multimedia types online, and new ones are being invented all the time. Learning the names of all the multimedia file types won't really help you; only through trial and error can you truly learn what your browser can't handle:

- When you open a page containing inline multimedia your browser can't handle, a message appears, telling you the name or type of file your browser can't play. Usually, you can still browse the page with no problem—you simply won't see or hear some of its multimedia.

- When you click a link leading to a type of external multimedia file your browser can't handle, a message usually appears to tell you the browser doesn't know what to do with the file. Often, the message offers a choice between canceling the download of the file or continuing the download, in case you want to save the file and play it later in another program.

The more up-to-date your browser program, the more types of multimedia it can handle.

Whenever you learn the file type of a multimedia file your browser can't play, you need to install a plug-in or helper application to add support for that file type (if that file type matters to you). You'll learn how to do that in Part 3. Until then, just browse around and see what happens. You may find that your browser already knows how to do nearly everything you want it to.

Cheat Sheet

Creating Shortcuts to Pages You Like

For pages you visit often, create a menu of shortcuts—called Bookmarks in Navigator and Favorites in Internet Explorer—that lead to those pages. To add a page to the menu, you go to that page, then

- In Navigator, click the Bookmarks button on the toolbar, and click Add Bookmark.
- In Internet Explorer 4, choose Favorites, Add to Favorites from the menu bar, then click OK.

To use an item in your list:

- In Navigator, click the Bookmarks button on the toolbar, and click the bookmark for the page you want to visit.
- In Internet Explorer 4, choose Favorites from the menu bar, then click the favorite for the page you want to visit.

Managing Your Shortcut List

Browsers that let you create a shortcut list also supply a dialog box on which you can delete and rename the shortcuts, and organize them in folders, to keep your list manageable.

Reliving Your History

Browsers feature a button or menu item for opening a list of pages you've visited recently—a history list—so you can easily return to them.

Printing and Saving Pages

You can save information from a Web page by printing it or saving it as a file on your computer, so you needn't revisit the page when you need that information again.

9

Getting Back to Places You Like

There are millions of Web pages, and only one of you. Even though you're special, if you're at least a little bit like most people, your Web surfing will eventually settle into a pattern wherein you revisit certain favorite pages often. And if you revisit certain pages often, you need convenient ways to get there. Here they are.

Basic Survival

Creating Shortcuts to Pages You Like

Most browsers let you build and maintain a list of shortcuts to pages you plan to revisit often.

While viewing a page you know you'll want to revisit, you can create a shortcut to it so any time you want to visit that page, you needn't type (or even remember!) its URL—all you do is choose the page's name from a menu, and your browser takes you there.

These shortcuts have two names:

- They're called bookmarks in Netscape Navigator.
- They're called favorites in Internet Explorer.

Folders help keep your shortcuts menu from getting too long.

To better organize your shortcuts, you can organize them in folders. Clicking a folder opens a submenu from which you can select a shortcut or another folder.

Adding a New Bookmark or Favorite

Before creating a new bookmark or favorite, you go to the particular page for which you want to make a bookmark or favorite. Once there, choose a button or menu item to create the shortcut.

To create a bookmark in Navigator:

1. Go to the page for which you want to create a bookmark.

2. Click the Bookmarks button on the toolbar.

3. In the menu, click Add Bookmark.

The new bookmark is added to your list; its name in the list is the title of the Web page it points to.

You can edit a bookmark (as described later) to rename it.

To create a favorite in Internet Explorer 4:

1. Go to the page you want to create a favorite for.

2. From the menu bar, choose Favorites, Add to Favorites

The name of the current page appears in a text box. That's the page title, and also the name that will appear in your favorites list. If the name shown is not descriptive enough to help you remember which page the favorite points to, you can optionally type a new name in the dialog box.

3. Make sure the top option button (next to No, just add the page to my favorites) is selected.

4. Click OK.

IE4's subscrip-
tions are not
recommended
for users of
dial-up connec-
tions because
they can
severely slow
performance.

The second and third option buttons on Internet Explorer's Add Favorite dialog box are for *sub-scribing* to Web pages and channels. Subscriptions automatically deliver selected Web page content to your computer at regular intervals, or whenever there's news.

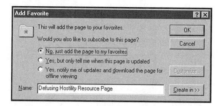

Going Where a Bookmark or Favorite Leads

From the moment you create a new favorite or bookmark, it appears as an item in the Bookmarks or Favorites menu. To use bookmarks and favorites, just open the menu and choose an item from the list.

- To display Navigator's Bookmarks list, click the Bookmarks button on the toolbar.

- To display Internet Explorer's Favorites list, choose Favorites from the menu bar.

When fin-
ished using
Favorites in
the Explorer
Bar, you can
close it by
clicking the
Close (X)
button in its
upper-right
corner.

In Internet Explorer 4, as an alternative to clicking Favorites on the menu bar, you can click the Favorites button in the toolbar to display your favorites list in the Explorer Bar. The Explorer Bar is a panel in the left side of the window that can display your Favorites list, plus other kinds of lists.

Explorer Bar

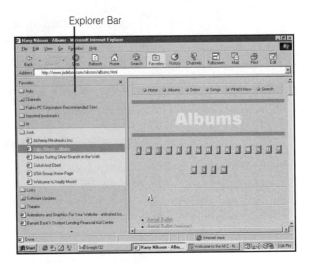

Beyond Survival

Managing Your Shortcut List

Over time, your list of shortcuts can become too long and unwieldy. To make it more manageable, you can delete bookmarks and favorites you no longer use, or you can organize them into folders.

You manage your shortcuts in a simple dialog box that lets you delete, move, or rename bookmarks and favorites much as you would any group of file icons in a Windows or Mac folder.

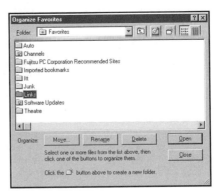

To manage shortcuts:

- In Internet Explorer 4, choose Favorites, Organize Favorites from the menu bar. Single-click a favorite you want to change to select it. To delete the selected favorite, click the Delete button. To move it into a folder, click the Move button, then click the folder in which you want to store the favorite, then click OK.

- In Navigator 4, click the Bookmarks button in the toolbar, then choose Edit Bookmarks. To delete a bookmark, single-click it to select it, then press the Delete key. To move a bookmark into a folder, click it and hold the mouse button down, drag to the folder, and release. To undo a mistake you make when editing bookmarks, choose Edit, Undo.

For shortcuts you want *really* fast access to, you can put a button right on a toolbar so clicking the button takes you straight to where the shortcut points:

- In Navigator 4, any bookmark you move into the Personal Toolbar folder appears as a button on Navigator's Personal toolbar.

- In Internet Explorer 4, any favorite you move into the Links folder appears as a button on the Links toolbar.

Reliving Your History

Bookmarks and favorites are the best way to go back where you've been. But suppose you want to revisit a page you didn't create a shortcut to, and you can't remember the URL. How can you find it?

To help you get back to those, browsers keep a record of where you've been: your history file. To revisit any page you've visited lately, open your browser's history file, locate an entry describing the page, and choose that entry.

Note that the history file keeps track of where you've been, no matter how you got there. Every time you go to a page—whether you get there by URL, link, bookmark, or favorite—the visit is recorded in your history file.

To use the history file:

- In Internet Explorer 4, click the History button, or choose View, Explorer Bar, History. The list opens in the Explorer Bar, a panel on the left side of the window. Click the folder for the day or week in which you last visited the site you're looking for, to display a list of recently visited sites. Click a site to display a list of pages visited on that site. Click a page to go there.

When finished using History in the Explorer Bar, you close it by clicking the Close (X) button in its upper-right corner.

- In Navigator 4, choose Communicator, History (or Window, History, in some versions). Sites are listed by time and date you visited them (from most recent to oldest). Scroll to the site you want, and double-click it to go there.

Browsers don't track your history forever; you'd wind up with a huge, unmanageable history file. Instead, browsers automatically delete all history file entries older than a set number of days.

By default, Navigator 4 deletes all history entries more than 9 days old; Internet Explorer deletes those older than 20 days. In either program, however, you can change the number of days the browser holds onto history entries:

- In Internet Explorer 4, choose View, Internet Options, General.

- In Netscape Navigator 4, choose Edit, Preferences, then choose Navigator from the list that appears in the left side of the dialog box.

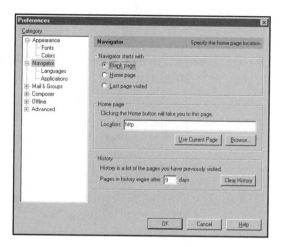

Recalling URLs You've Typed

Your history file keeps every page you've visited, no matter how you got there. But in addition to the history file, some browsers keep a separate list of every URL you've typed in the address box. This list makes retrieving and reusing a URL you've typed much easier.

You can take advantage of this list in either of two ways:

- **Drop-down list.** At the far-right end of the address box, you'll see an arrow. Click the arrow, and a list of URLs you've typed drops down. To visit any of the URLs listed, click it in the list.

Not all browsers feature a drop-down address list and AutoComplete.

- **AutoComplete.** Begin typing the URL in the address box. After you've typed enough of the URL for the browser to guess which URL you're typing, the browser fills in the rest of the URL in the address box. For example, if you've previously typed www.monkeys.com, and that URL is the only one in the list that begins "www.mo," you need type only that much of the URL in the address box—the rest suddenly appears. (If the suggestion is wrong, just keep typing and it goes away.)

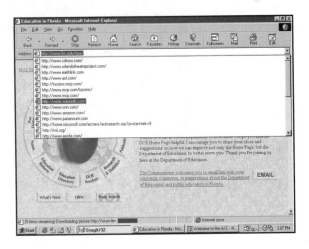

Practice Recalling Typed URLs

The following steps work in either Navigator 4 or Internet Explorer 4:

1. In your address box, enter the URL

   `www.habitat.org`

   and learn about the good work Habitat for Humanity does.

2. Using URLs, links, or shortcuts, browse away from Habitat for Humanity.

3. Drop down your address box list, and choose `www.habitat.org`. You return to Habitat.

4. Browse away from Habitat again.

5. In your address box, start typing `www.habitat.org` slowly. By the time you've typed as far as "www.h" or maybe "www.hab," the rest of the URL appears in the address box.

6. Press Enter to return to Habitat.

Printing and Saving Pages

Finally, there's the amazingly low-tech way of returning to a Web page: Don't.

You revisit a Web page because you expect its content to have changed, because you want news. But for information that doesn't change, there's no reason to keep going back to the Web page. Instead, save that information in a form you can consult offline, anytime.

To work offline in your browser, open it, then cancel the connection program.

The easiest way to do that is to print Web pages. In most browsers, that's as easy as clicking a Print button on the toolbar, or choosing Print from a menu (usually the File menu).

Alternatively, you can save Web pages on your hard disk. On the File menu of most browsers, you'll find a Save As item. Choose that, and you can save the current Web page as a file on your hard disk.

When you save a page, you usually save only its text; pictures aren't saved.

You can then open and view the page in your browser anytime, offline. To open a saved Web page, just double-click its file icon; it opens in your browser automatically (offline, of course).

Cheat Sheet

About Forms

A form is an area in a Web page where you can fill in information to send back to the Web server. Forms are the one part of Web browsing where you really need to be careful about your privacy, because forms may send information about you to the Web.

Forms use familiar objects for collecting information from you, such as:

- Text boxes. An empty box where you can type something.
- Lists. A list of choices, in which you click an item to select it.
- Check boxes. A small square beside an option in a form is a check box. You click it to put a check mark in it.
- Radio buttons. A small circle beside an option in a form is a radio button. Click it to fill it in.

After completing a form, you click a Submit button to send the form entries to the server.

Why Are Forms Risky?

Some forms ask you to enter such potentially sensitive information as your name, email address, social security number, or telephone number. You can often enter such information safely, but you must think twice about the security of the Web site and the integrity of the site's owner before submitting such information.

Identifying a Secure Site

Some Web sites that collect information through forms employ a security system in which information you send is scrambled when traveling between you and the server. Scrambling prevents prying by a third party. Such sites are called secure sites; sites that do not use a security system are called unsecure sites.

Recent versions of Internet Explorer and Netscape Navigator show you whether a site you're viewing is a secure site or not by displaying a padlock icon:

A locked padlock [image] indicates a secure site.

An unlocked padlock [image] (or no padlock) indicates an unsecure site.

10

Protecting Your Privacy

You may hear a lot on the news about how dangerous the Internet can be. Because you're reading this, you're brave enough to go online anyway, even if you're a little concerned. (I like that about you.) Although there are a few online pitfalls to watch out for, most of the stuff you hear about danger online is hype, and the few real risks are easily avoidable.

Basic Survival

About Forms

One important Web browsing technique I haven't shared with you yet is filling in online *forms*. A form is an area in a Web page where you can supply information that will be sent back to the Web server.

In Parts 7 and 8, you learn more about protecting your privacy in non-Web areas, such as Chat.

I had a reason to stall: Forms are the one part of Web browsing where you really need to be careful about your privacy.

You'll practice filling in a form later in this chapter, after I've explained the security issues you must consider before using a form.

For now, I'll tell you that filling in an online form is pretty much like filling in any form in any Windows or Mac program. Many of the same methods are used for making selections or typing entries, such as:

- Text boxes. An empty box where you can type something. You just click in the box, and type.

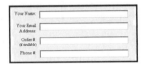

- Lists. A list of choices, in which you click an item to select it. Some lists work like Windows drop-down lists; you have to click an arrow on the list box to display the choices.

Check box and radio button parts of a form often have one item preselected, but you can change that choice.

- Check boxes. A small square beside an option in a form is a check box. You click it to put a check mark in it, which selects the item next to it. To remove the check mark, click the check box again.

- Radio buttons (sometimes called option buttons). A small circle next to an option in a form is a radio button. Click it to fill it in (make it a black circle), which selects or enables the item next to it. To deselect a radio button, click it again.

When you finish making all your entries and selections in a form, you must then send that information to the server.

Before you click the submit button, you may also go back and change any form entries.

A button always appears near the form, usually labeled "Submit," "Send," or "Done." (I'll just call it the submit button from here on, as long as you remember that it's not always labeled that way.) When you click the submit button, your form entries are sent to the server.

Nothing you do in a form goes to the server until you click the submit button. You can fill in all or part of a form, and as long as you don't click the submit button, you can jump to another page or go offline, and not a word is sent to the server.

Why Are Forms Risky?

Usually, when you visit a Web site, you *retrieve* information from the server, but you don't *send* anything about yourself to the server. You can browse all you like, and you're basically anonymous.

When you fill in a form, however, you send the information you supplied in the form to the server. Most of the time that's perfectly safe because the information you're sending isn't anything private.

For example, as you learn in Part 4, "Finding Web Sites," you perform most Internet searches by typing a *search term*—a word or two related to what you're looking for—in a simple form. A search term doesn't reveal much about you.

However, some forms want more from you, including such potentially sensitive information as

- Your name
- Your email address
- Your mailing address or telephone number
- Your credit card number
- Your Social Security number

Most often, a form collects this information when you're making a purchase. (You'll learn more about online shopping in Chapter 35, "Shopping Online.") If you join some sort of online organization or club, you may also be prompted to supply detailed information about yourself.

To make the most of the Web, you can't remain totally private; sooner or later, you're probably going to fill in a form with information about yourself. But before filling in any form, ask yourself three very important questions:

- Is the information requested by the form really necessary? Some forms collect more information from you than is really required. Don't feel like you must fill in every blank. Include only as much information as you are comfortable sharing. If the form requires you to fill in blanks you don't want to, consider whether the benefits of the form are worth the exposure.

When the info is more sensitive, be more careful; you can be freer with an email address than with a phone number.

- Do I trust the owners of this site with the information I'm providing? Is the site operated by a known company, one you trust, or is it a company you've never heard of? Just as you would over the telephone, think twice about whom you're dealing with before revealing anything about yourself.

- Is the site secure? Sending information to a secure site (described in the next section) decreases the risk—but it doesn't eliminate it.

About Secure Sites

Online criminals—called hackers—can collect credit card numbers and other information by intercepting it on its way from users like you to a Web server. This nasty trick is called data harvesting.

Some Web sites that collect information through forms (especially sites that sell online) employ a security system in which information you send is scrambled when traveling between you and the server, which prevents harvesting by a third party. Such sites are called secure sites; sites that do not use a security system are called unsecure sites.

Secure sites protect you from third parties—but you can still get stung if the site's owner is a crook!

To use the security systems built into secure sites, your browser must be compatible with the security systems used; the current versions of both Internet Explorer and Navigator are compatible with the systems used by secure sites today.

Identifying a Secure Site

Most browsers show you whether a page you're viewing is on a secure site or not:

- Internet Explorer displays a locked padlock at the bottom of the window (near the center) when you're communicating with a secure site. The lock does not appear at all when you're on an unsecure site.

- In Communicator (Navigator 4), a tiny padlock appears in the lower-left corner of the window. When the padlock appears to be unlocked, you are not connected to a secure site. When the padlock is locked, the site is secure.

- In versions of Navigator before 4.0, a tiny, gold key appears in the bottom of the browser window. When the key appears to be broken, you are not connected to a secure site. When the key appears intact, the site is secure.

"Secure" site = "encrypted" site.

In addition to little locks and keys, most browsers also have a fail-safe: They display a warning message before you send information to an unsecure site, so you have a chance to cancel (if you want) before actually sending anything.

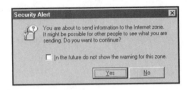

Beyond Survival

**Filling in a
Form**

Now that you know what to watch out for, you can safely complete an online form. For practice, fill out an online survey. (Note that Web pages change, and come and go, so there's no guarantee that the form below will look the same—or even be there—when you arrive. But it's worth a try...)

*You can
practice
without
actually
sending in the
survey—you'll
learn how in
a moment.*

1. Go to the MacMillian Computer Publishing Web site at
www.mcp.com.

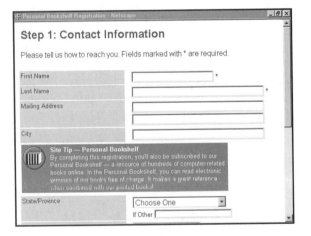

2. Click the link to Personal Bookself.

3. Click the link to Register Now! to open the form.

4. Fill in the information and click Continue at the bottom of the the form.

5. Answer all the questions in Step 2, then click Continue at the bottom of the form.

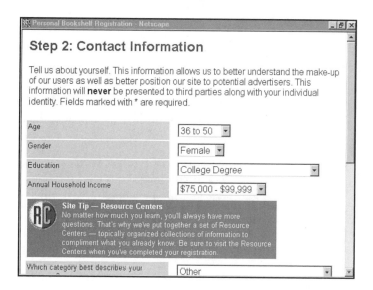

6. Answer the questions for Step 3, including the checkboxes.

This form is not secure—but that's okay, because you're not revealing anything personal.

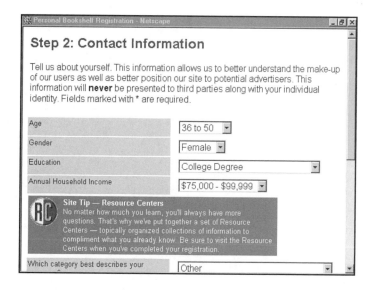

7. Add your comments or ideas in the Comment box.

8. Scroll back using the Back button, checking your answers and changing any you want to.

Now...

If you really want to go ahead and submit the survey, locate the Submit Survey button at the bottom of the form, and click it. After a few moments, a message appears to confirm that you are now registered and have subscribed to the Personel Bookshelf.

If you don't want to submit the form, just jump from this page to anywhere else (you can use Back, a Favorite or bookmark, or enter a URL). Because you left the form page without clicking the Continue button, you sent nothing to the server.

PART

3

Making Your Browser Do More

So much depends on your browser. Your browser must know how to access Web servers and display the Web pages and multimedia it finds there.

But on top of all that, your browser must be *extensible*; that is, it must have the capability to be refitted somehow to deal with file types and programs it was never designed for, all because petulant teenage geniuses keep inventing new file types and putting them online. Finally, a browser must let you customize the ways it protects you online, so that it doesn't protect you more or less aggressively than you want it to. In this part, you learn about ways you can customize and extend your browser, including

- Setting Your Browser's Security Options
- Adding Plug-Ins to Your Browser
- Using Helper Programs

Cheat Sheet

Knowing Whom You're Dealing With: Certificates

A certificate is a dialog box that appears when you enter some Web sites (or when that site sends program code, called a *script*, to you to enable an advanced function) to certify the identity of the site and its owner.

When a certificate appears, your browser usually presents you with a few options for dealing with it: You can accept the certificate (to interact with the site) or reject it.

Customizing Security in Navigator 4

To open Navigator's security dialog box, from the menu bar choose Communicator, Security Info (or Window, Security Info, if you use Navigator but not the full Communicator suite).

Customizing Security in Internet Explorer 4

To open Internet Explorer's security settings, choose View, Internet Options to open the Internet Options dialog box, and then click the Security tab.

To change the security level for a zone:

1. Open the Security tab (choose View, Internet Options, Security).
2. In the Zone list, select the zone for which you want to change security.
3. Select the security level you want.
4. Click OK.

Controlling Cookies

A *cookie* is a small amount of information a server stores on your computer for later reference. Cookies are usually harmless, and often useful. But you can customize either of the Big Two browsers to accept or reject all cookies, or to let you accept or reject each cookie on a case-by-case basis.

11

Setting Your Browser's Security Options

Most browsers let you customize the way they handle security. You can often choose when a browser displays warnings, which sites can run Java or other program code on your computer, and more. The settings your browser came with—its *default* settings—are probably fine as-is. Knowing how to fine-tune those settings, however, is an important part of taking control of your own safety online.

Basic Survival

Knowing Whom You're Dealing With: Certificates

If you use Navigator or Internet Explorer, now and then you'll come across a *certificate* on the Web. A certificate is a dialog box that appears when you enter some Web sites to certify the identity of the site and its owner. Certificates provide assurance that you're actually communicating with the company you think you're communicating with.

When you first see one, it seems like a big deal, but it's not. You won't see certificates often, and when you do, you can deal with them in just a click or two.

Certificates appear when you enter a site, or when the site wants to send you a program to enable a special function.

The exact options differ depending on the certificate.

Because a certificate positively identifies the company you're communicating with, you can better decide whether to accept program code, send your credit card or other info, or do anything else that might expose you to risk.

When a certificate appears, your browser usually presents you with a few options for dealing with it: You can accept the certificate (to interact with the site) or reject it.

Customizing Security in Navigator 4

To open Navigator's security dialog box, choose Communicator, Security Info (or Window, Security Info, if you use Navigator but not the full Communicator suite) from the menu bar.

When the dialog box opens, it shows any security information pertinent to the site you're currently viewing, such as whether the site is secure and whether any certificates are in force.

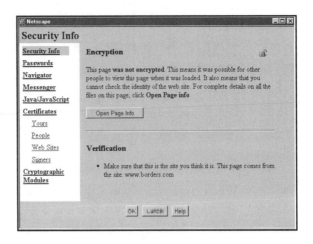

For maximum security, make sure all check boxes in the security dialog box are checked.

On the left side of the dialog box, a list of items for which you can customize security appears. In the list, click Navigator.

Use the check boxes and lists in the Navigator security dialog box to choose when warnings should appear. To learn more about what each setting means, click the dialog box's Help button.

Java and JavaScript are types of script code some sites run in your browser to enable special capabilities.

To control whether servers can run Java or JavaScript code on your computer, open Navigator's Preferences dialog box (choose Edit, Preferences) and click Advanced in the list on the left side of the dialog box. A dialog box opens in which you can select or deselect check boxes to enable or disable Java and JavaScript.

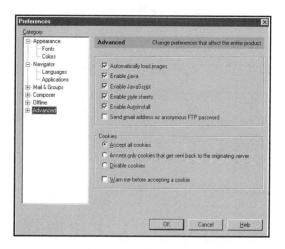

Customizing Security in Internet Explorer 4

To open Internet Explorer's security settings, choose View, Internet Options to open the Internet Options dialog box, and then click the Security tab.

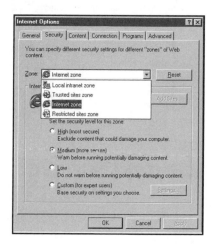

Internet Explorer's security system divides all sites into four different security zones:

- Local intranet zone. Includes all pages on your local intranet, if you have one. An intranet is an internal, private network, usually a company network that looks and acts like the Internet but isn't open to the outside world.

- Trusted sites zone. Includes Web sites you have selected as "trusted" sites, those for which you may want less strict security than others.

- Internet zone. All Internet Web sites that you have not included in your Trusted sites zone or your Restricted sites zone.

- Restricted sites zone. Sites you don't particularly trust, generally ones for which you want higher security than for other zones.

If your computer is not on a company network, you can ignore the Local intranet zone.

Using the Security tab, you can add sites to your Trusted sites and Restricted sites zones, and choose security settings for each of the four zones.

Adding a Site to a Zone in Internet Explorer

1. Open the Security tab (choose View, Internet Options, Security tab).

2. In the Zone list, select the zone to which you want to add sites.

3. Click the Add Sites button. A dialog box opens, showing the URLs of sites already in the zone.

4. In the text box at the bottom of the dialog box, type the URL of a site you want to add to the zone, then click Add to add it to the list.

Beyond Survival

Understanding Zone Security Settings

The security settings for a zone determine how aggressive the security system in Internet Explorer will be when communicating with Web sites in that zone.

100

For example, you can always view pages on any site, regardless of security settings. Within a zone for which high security is in effect, however, if a server attempts to send a script or other program code that could give your computer a virus or other problem, Internet Explorer prevents the code from reaching your computer.

The security levels you can assign to zones are

To totally block access to particular sites, use Internet Explorer's Content Advisor, as described in Chapter 34, "Tips for Parents."

- High. All potentially damaging content (such as scripts) is automatically refused.

- Medium. Internet Explorer prompts you before accepting any potentially damaging content, giving you the opportunity to accept or reject it.

- Low. Open the gates. Internet Explorer accepts anything.

By default, each of the four zones has a reasonable security setting: High for restricted sites, Medium for the Local intranet and Internet zones, and Low for trusted sites.

If you get tired of being prompted every time an Internet page sends some Java to your computer, you might want to change the security level for the Internet zone to low. Conversely, if you've experienced a lot of problems with Java, you might want to apply high security to the whole Internet zone. If you trust your coworkers, you might want to change your Local intranet zone to low security.

To change the security level for a zone:

1. Open the Security tab (choose View, Internet Options, Security).

2. In the Zone list, select the zone for which you want to change security.

3. Select the security level you want.

4. Click OK.

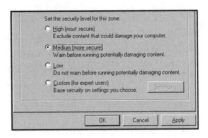

Understanding Cookies

Besides scripts, servers can put another thing on your computer you may not know about: *cookies.*

A cookie is a small amount of information a server stores on your computer for later reference. Typically, a server stores an identifying code of some sort on your computer so it can automatically identify you any time you visit the site. That saves you the time of telling the server who you are.

Cookies are usually harmless, and often useful. For example, an online store from which you've purchased once may put a cookie on your computer that identifies you. Any time you return to that site to shop, the server automatically knows who you are, and you needn't bother filling in a form to identify yourself.

Your computer is your domain, however, and you get to decide what someone else can put there. You can customize either of the Big Two browsers to accept or reject cookies.

Controlling Cookies in Navigator

1. Open Navigator's Preferences dialog box by choosing Edit, Preferences.

2. In the list along the left side of the dialog box, click Advanced. The Advanced dialog box opens.

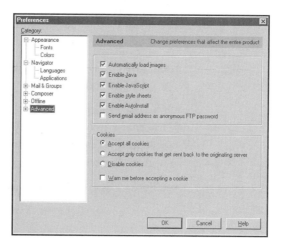

3. In the bottom of the dialog box, choose how you want cookies handled:

- Choose Accept all cookies to automatically accept any cookie.

- Choose Accept only cookies that get sent back to the originating server to accept most cookies, but to reject any that might be readable by servers other than the one who sent you the cookies. This prevents cookies on your computer from being read by any server other than the cookie's creators.

- Choose Disable cookies to reject all cookies.

- Check the Warn me before accepting a cookie check box if you want Navigator to display a dialog box before accepting a cookie, and to offer you buttons for optionally accepting or rejecting the cookie.

Controlling Cookies in Internet Explorer

1. Open the Internet Options dialog box (choose View, Internet Options).

2. Click the Advanced tab. The Advanced tab presents a long list of items you can enable or disable with check boxes and radio buttons.

3. Scroll down to the Security section of the list, and find the Cookies choices at the bottom of the Security section.

- Choose Always accept cookies to automatically accept any cookie.

- Choose Prompt before accepting cookies to instruct Internet Explorer to display a dialog box before accepting a cookie, and to offer you buttons for optionally accepting or rejecting the cookie.

- Choose Disable all cookie use to reject all cookies.

Cheat Sheet

Understanding How Browsers Are Enhanced

Web browsers can be reprogrammed through the Web to acquire new capabilities. This happens through three types of program files:

- Plug-ins
- Scripts
- ActiveX files

Finding Plug-Ins

Usually, when you come across a Web site or a file that requires a particular plug-in, it's accompanied by a link for downloading the plug-in. Occasionally, you have to go plug-in hunting. The first stop is Netscape at `home.netscape.com/plugins/`.

Another source is the Plug-In Plaza at `browserwatch.internet.com/plug-in.html`.

A third plug-in resource is the Plug-in Gallery & Demo Links page at `www2.gol.com/users/oyamada/`.

Installing and Using Plug-Ins

Because plug-ins can come from any software publisher, no single method exists for installing them. Typically, you have to run some sort of installation program, and then specify the directory in which your Web browser is installed. Carefully read any instructions you see, click the link, and follow any prompts that appear.

Important Plug-Ins to Have

Begin exploring with your browser just as it comes, and install plug-ins only as they become necessary. However, you should consider getting two plug-ins right away because they're so commonly used on the Web.

The first is the RealAudio player at `www.realaudio.com`.

The other you'll soon need is Shockwave at `www.macromedia.com`.

12

Adding Plug-Ins to Your Browser

The most important enhancements to browsers come as *plug-ins*, which are easy to find, download, and install in your browser. In this chapter, you learn about plug-ins, plus a few other important browser power extenders.

Basic Survival

Understanding How Browsers Are Enhanced

The two most popular Web browsers, Navigator and Internet Explorer, can be reprogrammed through the Web to acquire new capabilities. This happens through three types of program files:

- Plug-ins. A plug-in is a program that implants itself in the browser to add a new capability. After you install a plug-in, usually that new capability appears to be a native, built-in part of the browser, as if it had always been there.

- Scripts (Java, JavaScript). Both browsers support programs, called scripts, written in the Java and JavaScript languages (and sometimes other languages, such as VBScript), that are used to enable advanced multimedia, forms, and other cool stuff on leading-edge Web pages.

- ActiveX files. An ActiveX-enabled file includes program code that teaches the browser how to display it. Internet Explorer has support for ActiveX files built-in. Navigator requires an ActiveX plug-in to handle ActiveX files.

You can get the ActiveX plug-in for Navigator at www. ncompasslabs .com

In general, you don't have to do anything special to take advantage of scripts or ActiveX; they're delivered to the browser automatically by Web sites. More often than not, however, you must deliberately download and install a particular plug-in to enjoy whatever it does.

Finding Plug-Ins

Usually when you come across a Web site or a file that requires a particular plug-in, it's accompanied by a link for downloading the plug-in. In fact, when first entering the site, a message may appear on your screen, informing you that a particular plug-in is required, and giving you a link for downloading it.

Occasionally, however, the site doesn't help you get the right plug-in, and you have to go plug-in hunting.

Fortunately, several excellent indexes are devoted to plug-ins. The first stop is Netscape, where a full directory of plug-ins is maintained, along with links to the latest, coolest ones to come out. You can reach Netscape's Plug-Ins index at

```
home.netscape.com/plugins/
```

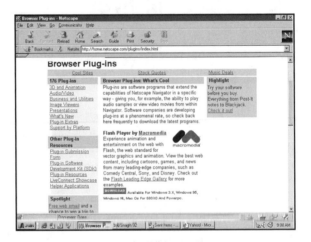

Another good source is the Plug-In Plaza at

```
browserwatch.internet.com/plug-in.html
```

This page has an extensive list of all available plug-ins, as well as the companies creating the plug-ins.

From the site's top page, you can view the plug-ins by type (multimedia, graphics, sounds, and so on) or by platform (Windows, Macintosh, UNIX, and OS/2). Just select the listing type you want and scroll through the list to see what's available. You can download the plug-in directly from this page or visit the developer and read the latest news about the plug-in.

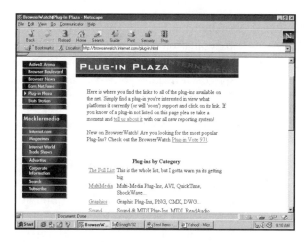

A third plug-in resource is the Plug-in Gallery & Demo Links page at

www2.gol.com/users/oyamada/

You can view the list of plug-ins for certain types of applications, such as video players and image viewers. Or, if you're looking for a particular plug-in, just click the list for that type, and select the name of the plug-in you're looking for.

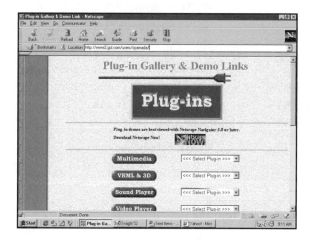

Installing and Using Plug-Ins

Because plug-ins can come from any software publisher, no single method exists for installing them. Typically, you have to run some sort of installation program, and then specify the directory in which your Web browser is installed.

When you come across a link to a plug-in, carefully read any instructions you see, click the link, and follow any prompts that appear. You'll do fine.

Although there's no standard method of installing plug-ins, using them is pretty much the same. Because they work with the browser, you never really see the plug-in. Often, a plug-in adds to your browser a few new menu items or toolbar buttons that are useful when dealing with the type of file the plug-in handles.

Some plug-ins can install into multiple browsers, so you can access the tool no matter which browser you use.

Beyond Survival

Important Plug-Ins to Have

In general, you should begin exploring with your browser just as it comes, and install plug-ins only as they become necessary. However, you should consider getting two plug-ins right away because they're so broadly exploited on the Web.

The first is the RealAudio player, which you'll find at

        www.realaudio.com

The RealAudio player enables your browser to play live audio feeds, from radio broadcasts to news updates to live music. The RealAudio home page also provides links to fun places where you can try out RealAudio.

On the RealAudio site, you can also get a plug-in for playing inline video delivered in RealVideo format.

110

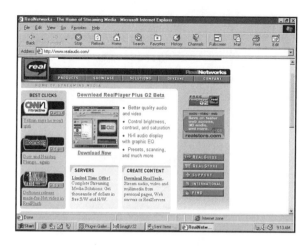

The other enhancement you'll soon need is Shockwave, from Macromedia, at

www.macromedia.com

A set of plug-ins that install and work together, Shockwave enables your browser to play what are called "shocked sites," pages featuring highly interactive multimedia. The Macromedia site also features fun links to cool shocked sites.

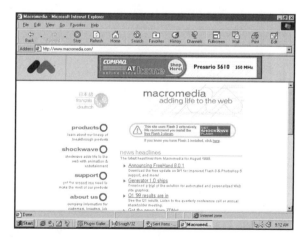

Another important plug-in is the QuickTime player. That program equips Navigator or Internet Explorer to play video clips stored in .MOV format, of which there are many online.

111

If you have a Mac or your PC has a QuickTime player, the browser may use the existing player as a helper (see Chapter 13, "Using Helper Programs").

This free player is not quite as critical as the two I just mentioned, however, because the Mac includes native support for QuickTime files, and most Windows systems already have a QuickTime player installed automatically by many multimedia CD-ROM programs.

If you have trouble playing a .MOV video, however, get the plug-in at

```
quicktime.apple.com
```

Cheat Sheet

Adding Helpers to Older Browsers

Browsers other than Navigator and Internet Explorer often rely on separate helper programs to deal with some file types, because the browsers usually support few file types natively and almost never can be enhanced by plug-ins.

In these browsers, you will find a dialog box that lists the helper program assigned to each file type. You add helpers by installing them on your computer, then adding them to the list in your browser's dialog box.

Adding Helpers to Internet Explorer and Navigator

To install a new helper for Navigator or Internet Explorer, simply install the program itself on your computer. The installation routines for most programs automatically update the file types Registry to make the program the default for the file type it handles.

Examining the Windows Files Types Registry

To see which programs are assigned to which file types in Windows 95/98, open any folder and choose View, Options, File Types.

Examining Navigator's Helper Applications Dialog Box

Navigator 4 features an easy-to-find dialog box for viewing and editing the file Registry to update your helper program settings.

1. Choose Edit, Preferences.
2. Locate the word "Navigator" in the list along the left, and click the + sign next to Navigator.
3. Click Applications.

13

Using Helper Programs

Unlike plug-ins, helper programs don't work inside your browser. A helper program is any program on your computer that has been configured to handle a particular type of file—a picture, sound clip, document, whatever—that your browser can't handle itself. When the browser comes across such a file, it opens the helper program to get the job done.

For example, if you click a link that opens a text file (.txt) and your browser can't display text files on its own, it might open Windows' Notepad program in a separate window to show you the file. That's how helpers work.

Basic Survival

Adding Helpers to Older Browsers

Browsers other than the Big Two (Navigator and Internet Explorer)—and old versions of the Big Two, also—rely heavily on helpers, because the browsers usually support few file types natively and almost never can be enhanced by plug-ins.

In these browsers, you typically find a dialog box that lists the helper program assigned to each file type. You can add new helper programs by installing them on your computer, then adding them to the list in your browser's dialog box.

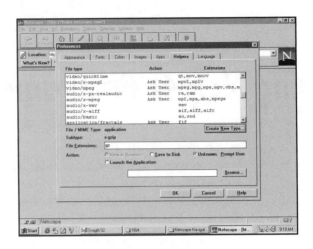

Adding Helpers to Internet Explorer and Navigator

The latest versions of the Big Two rarely rely on helpers, because they feature native support for so many file types and can use plug-ins for so many more. Both browsers can call on helpers, when necessary.

When they do need a helper, Navigator and Internet Explorer don't need to be configured to use helper programs; they make use of the Windows or Mac file types Registry. If Windows or the Mac system already has a program registered to automatically handle a given file type, that's the program the browser opens when you access that type of file.

In particular, the file types Registry keeps tally of the program to use for each MIME file type. MIME (multipurpose Internet mail extensions) is a standard that determines the file types for various objects that travel through the Internet, particularly such things as file attachments on email messages. Because the file types Registry has entries in it for each common MIME file type, Internet Explorer and Navigator always know what to do with any file you receive that falls under the MIME specification.

To install a new helper for Navigator or Internet Explorer, all you usually have to do is install the program itself on your computer. The installation routines for most programs automatically update the file types Registry to make the program the default for the file type it handles.

If you install a program and your browser fails to call upon it when necessary, you may need to work with the Registry (described next).

116

Beyond Survival

Examining the Windows File Types Registry

If you use Windows 95, 98, or NT, you can open your file types Registry to learn which programs are registered to handle which types of files. These are the programs Internet Explorer or Navigator will call upon to display files for which they have no native support or plug-in.

1. Open any folder and choose View, Options, File Types to open the File Types tab.

2. Scroll through the list and see which programs have been configured.

3. To see which extensions are associated with a particular program, click the program's name in the list.

Windows 98 users (and Windows 95 users with IE4) choose View, Folder Options, File Types.

Any change you make to the Registry affects not just Web browsing, but all of Windows.

Examining Navigator's Helper Applications Dialog Box

Navigator 4 features an easy-to-find dialog box for viewing and editing the file Registry to update your helper program settings.

1. In Navigator, choose Edit, Preferences.

2. In the dialog box that appears, locate the word "Navigator" in the list along the left side.

3. Click the + sign next to Navigator to display the choices below it. (To hide the choices again, click the –sign.)

The dialog box
is a new
view on file
Registry;
changes you
make affect
all of
Windows.

4. Click Applications. The file Registry opens.

5. To see which extensions are associated with a particular program, click the program's name in the list.

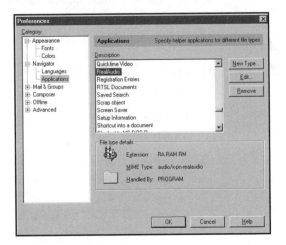

Finding Web Sites

There's just too much on the Web. It's like having a TV set with a billion channels; you could click the remote until your thumb fell off, and still never find the *Law & Order* reruns.

Fortunately, a number of search tools on the Web help you find exactly what you're looking for, anywhere on the Web, and even *beyond* the Web in other Internet arenas. In this part, you'll discover what searching the Web is all about, including

- Finding a Search Tool
- Clicking Through Categories
- Using Search Terms

Cheat Sheet

What Is a Search Tool?

A search tool is a Web page where you can conduct a search of the Web.

Where Are the Major Search Tools?

About a dozen general-purpose search tools are out on the Web; you can visit any search tool by entering its URL. To try a few:

- Go to Yahoo! at `www.yahoo.com`.
- Jump to Excite at `www.excite.com`.
- Jump to Alta Vista at `altavista.digital.com`.

Using Your Browser's Search Button

Most major browsers have a Search button on their toolbars, or a Search item somewhere within their menus. The Search button or menu item is preconfigured to take you to a particular search tool; it doesn't really help you search, it just makes opening a search tool convenient.

- In Navigator 4 (Communicator), clicking the Search button opens Netscape's all-in-one NetSearch page.
- In Internet Explorer 4, clicking the Search button opens a list of search tool options in the Explorer bar.

14

Finding a Search Tool

The first step to finding anything on the Web is knowing about the various search tools available online, and where to find them.

Basic Survival

What Is a Search Tool?

A search tool is a Web page where you can conduct a search of the Web. Such pages have been set up by a variety of companies who offer you free Web searching and support the service, at least in part, through the advertising you'll see prominently displayed on most search tool pages.

The term *search engine* is sometimes used to describe a search tool. But this term more accurately describes the program a search tool uses, behind the scenes, to perform searches. When you hear someone refer casually to a "search engine," just remember that they probably mean "search tool."

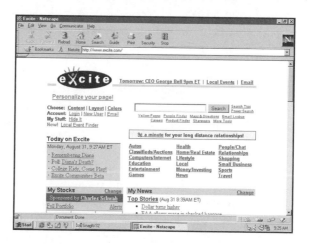

Although using the various search tools is similar, each has its own, unique search methods. But more important, each has its own, unique set of files—a *database*—upon which all searches are based.

You see, no search tool actually goes out and searches the entire Web when you ask it to. A search tool searches its own database of information about the Web. The more complete and accurate that database is, the more successful your searches are likely to be.

The database for a search tool is created in either (or both) of two ways:

- Manually. Folks who've created Web pages, or who've discovered pages they want the world to know about, fill in a form on the search tool's Web site to add new pages (and their descriptions) to the database.

- Through a crawler (or spider, or worm). All these creepy-crawly names describe programs that systematically contact Web servers (at regular intervals), scan the contents of the server, and add information about the contents of the server to the database. (They "crawl" around the Web, like "spiders"—get it?) It takes the crawler a few weeks to complete each of its information-gathering tours of the Web.

Where a search tool's database has been created by a crawler, the tool tends to deliver results that are more complete and up-to-date, whereas manually built databases tend to contain more meaningful categorization and more useful descriptive information.

Because search tools search a database and not the actual Web, they sometimes deliver results that are out-of-date. You may click a link that a search tool delivered to you, and find that the page to which it points no longer exists. That happens when a page has been removed since the last time the search tool's database was updated.

No two search tools turn up exactly the same results for any given topic—so try a few.

Despite differences and strengths and weaknesses among the available tools, the bottom line is this: Any of the major search tools may locate a page or pages that meet your needs; any may not. If you can't find what you want through one tool, try another.

Where Are the Major Search Tools?

About a dozen general-purpose search tools exist out on the Net, and many, many more specialized search tools are out there, too. You can visit any search tool by entering its URL.

Top Search Tools

Tool	URL
Yahoo!	www.yahoo.com
Excite	www.excite.com
Alta Vista	altavista.digital.com
Lycos	www.lycos.com
Infoseek	www.infoseek.com
Open Text	www.opentext.com
HotBot	www.hotbot.com
WebCrawler	www.webcrawler.com

Checking Out the Search Engines

Before beginning to use search tools, take a peek at a few. While visiting these pages, watch for helpful links that point to

- Instructions for using the search tool.

- A text box near the top of the page, which is where you'd type a search term.

- Links to categories you can browse (see Chapter 15, "Clicking Through Categories").

- Reviews and ratings of recommended pages.

- "Cool Sites"—a regularly updated, random list of links to especially fun or useful pages you may want to visit just for kicks.

- Links to other search engines.

You learn all about using search terms in Chapter 16, "Using Search Terms."

Try a little tour:

1. Go to Yahoo! at www.yahoo.com.

Observe that Yahoo! features a text box at the top (for a search term) and a table of categories below, for searching by category. Note also the graphical buttons at the top of the page, for displaying Cool Sites and such.

2. Jump to Excite at www.excite.com.

Observe that Excite also features a search term box and category headings.

3. Jump to Alta Vista at altavista.digital.com.

Which familiar search tool features do you see?

Category Headings   Search Term Box

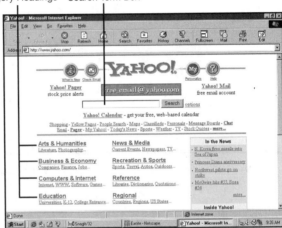

Beyond Survival

Using Your Browser's Search Button

Most major browsers (including Internet Explorer and Netscape Navigator) have a Search button on their toolbars, or a Search item somewhere within their menus. To use your browser's search features productively, you need to understand what they do.

In general, a Search button (or Search menu item) is preconfigured to take you to a particular search tool; the button doesn't really help you search, it just makes opening a search tool convenient.

The default home page configured in Communicator doubles as an all-in-one search page.

Some browser makers configure the Search buttons in their products to go to an "all-in-one" search page on the browser maker's Web site. An all-in-one search page lets you use several different search tools from the same page.

The page is not really a search tool itself; rather, it accepts your searching instructions, passes them on to a search tool, retrieves the results from the tool, and then displays them.

Using Navigator's Search Button

In Navigator 4 (Communicator), clicking the Search button opens Netscape's all-in-one search page.

Notice the row of buttons, each naming a search tool (Lycos, Yahoo!, Excite, Infoseek). To use one of those tools, you click the button, which opens that tool's search term box and other tools in the box below the buttons.

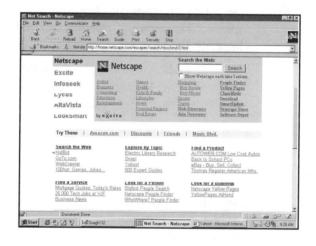

Using Internet Explorer 4's Search Button and Explorer Bar

Clicking the Search button on Internet Explorer 4's toolbar opens the Explorer bar, a pane in the left side of the browser window. The Explorer bar is also used in Internet Explorer for displaying your Favorites and History list (see Chapter 9, "Getting Back to Places You Like").

In the Explorer bar, the Provider-of-the-day (one of the major search tools picked daily, at random) appears automatically. You can use that tool, or click the drop-down list at the top of the Explorer bar to choose from among a few other tools, such as Excite or Yahoo!.

After you've picked a favorite search tool, make a favorite or bookmark for it (see Chapter 9).

No matter which tool you choose, anything you do with that tool—whether clicking through categories or using a search term—happens in the Explorer bar.

When you finally open a page from your search, that page appears in the main window, to the right of the Explorer bar. You can continue searching in the Explorer bar, or close the Explorer bar by clicking the Close (X) button in the Explorer bar's upper-right corner (that's the X in the left-hand pane, NOT the X at the extreme upper-right of the browser window, which closes the browser).

The Explorer bar can be a handy feature, but it can also be a pretty cramped place to work with a search tool. Always remember that you're not required to use the Search button; you can always enter a search tool's URL in Internet Explorer to work in that tool, full-screen.

Cheat Sheet

Why Use Categories Instead of a Search Term?

Foregoing search terms (see Chapter 16, "Using Search Terms") and clicking through a directory's categories is an effective way to find stuff and also a great way to become more familiar with what's available on the Web.

Also, the more broad your topic of interest, the more useful categories are, because broad search terms may deliver too many results to be useful.

Using a Directory

Begin on the search tool's top page, and click a category heading to display a list of related subcategories. Click a subcategory heading, and you display its list of secondary subcategories.

Continue drilling down through the directory structure until you arrive at a targeted list of links to pages related to a particular topic.

Smart Category Surfing

Many search tools feature special forms on subcategory or results pages that you can use to narrow or refine your search—perform a new search that looks only within the selected subcategory or results.

15

Clicking Through Categories

These days, all the major search tools accept *search terms* (see Chapter 16). But a few also supply a directory of categories—an index of sorts—that you can browse to locate links to pages related to a particular topic. Tools that feature such directories include Yahoo!, Excite, and Infoseek.

Basic Survival

Why Use Categories Instead of a Search Term?

When you're first becoming familiar with the Web, foregoing the search terms and clicking through a directory's categories is not only an effective way to find stuff but also a great way to become more familiar with what's available on the Web.

As you browse through categories, you inevitably discover detours to interesting topics and pages that you didn't set out to find. Exploring directories is an important part of learning how the Web works and what's on it.

Categories are better than search terms when your topic is broad.

Also, the broader your topic of interest, the more useful categories are. When you use a search term to find information related to a broad topic (cars, dogs, music, plants), the search tool typically delivers a bewildering list containing hundreds or thousands of pages. Some of these pages meet your needs, but many are pages that merely mention the topic rather than being about the topic.

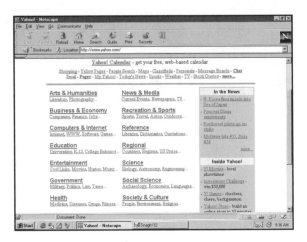

A search term usually delivers some links that match the term, but not your intentions; a search on "plant" will likely turn up not only botany and houseplant pages, but others about power plants, folks named Plant, and maybe the Plantagenet family of European lore. Categories, on the other hand, help you limit the results of your search to the right ballpark.

Using a Directory

Everything in a directory is a link; to find something in a directory, you follow those links in an organized way.

You begin by clicking a broad category heading to display a list of related subcategories. Click a subcategory heading, and you display its list of secondary subcategories.

You continue in this fashion, drilling down through the directory structure (usually through only two to five levels), until you eventually arrive at a targeted list of links to pages related to a particular topic.

After you finish with a page you jumped to, click your Back button to return to the list of pages and visit another.

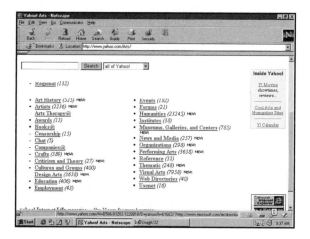

Exploring Categories

Try rooting around in Yahoo! to get a feel for using directories:

1. Go to Yahoo! at www.yahoo.com.

2. In the list of categories on the top page, click Entertainment. A list of Entertainment subcategories appears.

3. Click Amusement and Theme Parks. A list of related subcategories appears.

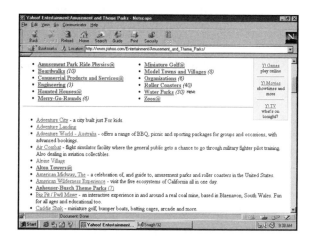

4. Scroll down below the subcategories, and you'll find some links leading to pages about amusement parks.

   You can click one of the subcategories to see more options, or visit one of the pages.

5. Click Back twice to return to the top Yahoo! page. Observe that you can try any path or page and then back out by as many levels as you want to so you can try a different path.

6. Explore on your own, clicking down through the directory and then back up again with Back.

You can use the Back button to go back up the directory tree, so you can try a different route.

Beyond Survival

Smart Category Surfing

With a little practice, you can develop smart ways to browse categories more effectively. One is to refine a search by doing a second search within the subcategory or results turned up by the first. (You learn more about using search terms like those here in Chapter 16.)

Notice that at the top of any search results page Yahoo! shows you a text box (for a new search term) and a list. From the list, you can choose:

• All of Yahoo!. Yahoo! will look for all instances of the search term in its whole database.

• Just this category. Yahoo! will look for instances of the search term only from within the records for the subcategories and sites in the results you're viewing.

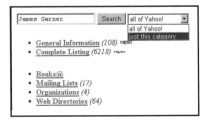

Try using a search term (see Chapter 16) to find a related subcategory listing, then click around the subcategory to find stuff.

For example, suppose you want info on an actor with a common name. If you use that name as a search term (see Chapter 16) from the top of Yahoo!, the results will include sites about the actor, but also lots of other sites about other people with the same name.

If you browse to the Actors and Actresses subcategory first, however, and then search for that name just within the category, the results should all relate to the actor—and *only* the actor.

Cheat Sheet

Understanding Searches

When you submit a search term, the search tool explores its database of information about Web pages, locating any entries that contain the same combination of characters in your search term.

The search tool then displays a list of links to all the pages it determined were matches: the *hit list*.

Phrasing a Simple Search

To submit a search term, go to the search tool, type a simple word or phrase in the text box, click the submit button, and wait a few moments for the hit list to show up. If the list shows links that look like they hold what you're after, try them. If not, try a new search with a different term.

When phrasing your search term, follow these guidelines:

- Use the simplest form of a word.
- Use common capitalization.
- Be as specific as possible.

What Is a Good Number of Hits?

Zero hits is a problem, but hundreds or even thousands of hits may be just fine. Most search engines put the best hits—the closest matches to your search term—at the top of the list.

If you don't see what you want somewhere in the first 30–50 links, you probably need to start over, with a new search term.

Using Multiple Words in a Search Term

In a search term, you can use as many words as you need to make the term specific.

Using Operators to Control Searches

An operator is a word or symbol used to specify the action in an equation, such as plus or minus. Operators are used in search terms to express a logical equation of sorts that tightly controls how a search engine handle's the term. There are three basic operators used in searching: and, or, and not.

16

Using Search Terms

Clicking categories, as you learned to do in Chapter 15, "Clicking Through Categories," can be a productive way to search. But often, a more powerful method is called for, one that delivers a custom-made list of links related to any topic you can imagine.

That's what search terms do. In this chapter, you learn how to use search terms, and how to phrase them carefully to produce precisely the results you need.

Basic Survival

Understanding Searches

Each of the search tools described in Chapters 14, "Finding a Search Tool," and 15, "Clicking Through Categories"—and just about any other you might encounter on the Web—has a text box featured prominently near the top of its main page. You type your search terms in that text box.

Search Term box

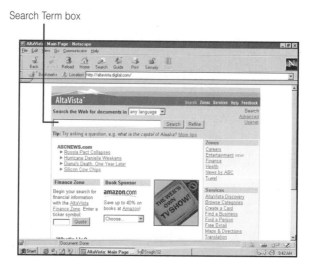

Adjacent to the box, there's always a submit button, almost always labeled "Search" Search but occasionally labeled something else, such as "Submit."

Such searches are sometimes also called keyword searches.

Typing a search term in a text box and then clicking the submit button to send the term to the search tool is known as submitting a search term.

When you submit a search term, the search tool explores its database of information about pages, locating any entries that contain the same combination of characters in your search term.

Although the contents of the various search tool databases differ, the record for each page typically contains the page's URL, title, a brief description, and a group of keywords intended to describe the page's contents. If your search term matches anything in that record, the search tool considers the page a match.

The list of links shown as the search results is often called a hit list.

After searching the whole database (which takes only a moment or two), the search tool displays a list of links to all the pages it determined were matches.

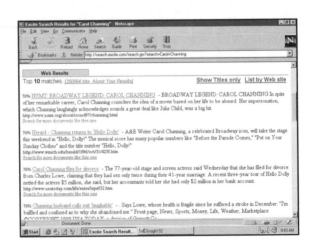

Each hit in the list is a link. You can scroll through the hit list, reading the page titles and descriptions to determine which page might best serve your needs, then click the link to that page to go there.

Some tools organize the hit list in smart ways, attempting to put the best matches at the top of the list so you see them first, and weaker matches lower in the list.

If a page you open from the hit list isn't what you're looking for, click Back to return to the hit list and try a different hit.

For example, suppose you use *Godzilla* as your search term. A particular search tool would tend to put at the top of the hit list all pages that use the word "Godzilla" in their titles or URLs, because those are the pages most likely to be all about Godzilla.

Matches to keywords or the page's description come lower in the list, because these may be pages that simply mention Godzilla, but aren't really *about* Godzilla. Even lower in the list, a tool might show links to "partial" matches, pages to which only part of the search term, such as those containing the word "God" or the partial word "zilla."

Phrasing a Simple Search

You can get awfully artful and creative with search terms, but nine times out of ten, you needn't get too fancy about searching. Go to the search tool, type a simple word or phrase in the text box, click the submit button, and wait a few moments for the hit list to show up. Cinch.

If the list shows links that look like they hold what you're after, try them. If not, try another search term.

Consider these basic tips for improving your search success:

When using such terms, obey goofy computer-era capitalizations, such as AppleTalk or FrontPage.

- Use the simplest form of a word. The search term Terrier will match references to both "Terrier" and "Terriers." However, the term Terriers may fail to match pages using only "Terrier." Some search tools are smart enough to account for this, but some aren't. So try to use the simplest word form that's still specific to what you want.

- Use common capitalization. Some search tools don't care about capitalization, but some do. So it's always a good habit to capitalize words as they are most often printed, using initial capitals on names and other proper nouns and all lowercase letters for other words.

- Be as specific as possible. If it's the "German Shepherd" you want to know about, use that as your search term, not "dog," which will produce too many hits, many unrelated to German Shepherds. If the most specific term doesn't get what you want, then try less specific terms; if German Shepherd fails, go ahead and try dog. You may find a generic page about dogs on which there's a link to information about German Shepherds.

- Try partial words. Always try full words first. But if they're not working out, you can use a partial word. If you want to match both "puppies" and "puppy," you can try "pup" as a search term, which matches both.

Try a simple search:

1. Go to Alta Vista at `altavista.digital.com`.

2. Locate the search term box, right in the middle of the page.

3. Click the search term box, and type: `DaVinci`.

4. Locate the submit button, which is below the search term box and labeled "search."

5. Click the Search button, and wait a few moments for the hit list to appear.

6. Examine the hit list. What kinds of pages does a search on DaVinci turn up in Alta Vista? Are they all about the artist/inventor, or are they about other stuff called "DaVinci," as well?

7. Choose any hit in the list, and click the link. The page to which it points appears.

8. Click your Back button to return to the hit list.

9. Scroll to the bottom of the page. Near the bottom, a row of buttons or links appears, one of which is a link for advancing to the next page in the hit list. In Alta Vista, this "next page" button looks like >>. (It'll look different in different tools, but it's usually pretty easy to spot.)

10. Click the next page button. The next page of hits appears.

When a search turns up more hits than can fit on one page, the hits are divided onto multiple pages.

11. Think of something you really want to know more about, and try a new search for what matters to *you*.

What Is a Good Number of Hits?

A hit list may show no hits at all, or it may show thousands. Zero hits is a problem, but hundreds or even thousands often isn't. Remember, most search engines put the best hits—the closest matches to your search term—at the top of the list.

Regardless of the number of hits, if you don't see what you want somewhere in the first 30–50 links, you probably need to start over with a new search term. If your first search turned up thousands of hits, use a more specific term in your second try.

At the bottom of each page of a hit list, links or buttons appear for moving to other hit list pages.

Beyond Survival

Using Multiple Words in a Search Term

In a search term, you can use as many words as you need to make the term specific.

For example, suppose I want to learn about Boxer dogs. I could use the search term *Boxer*. Although that term might turn up some hits about Boxer dogs, those hits may be buried among hundreds of other links about prizefighters, China's Boxer rebellion, Tony Danza (actor and ex-boxer), and people named Boxer.

So to make my search more specific, I use two words—"Boxer dog." Now the search engine looks for pages that contain both "Boxer" and "dog," which greatly increases the chances that hits will be about Boxer dogs, because most pages about all those

139

Even if the list has thousands of hits, the links you want may well appear somewhere within the top 20 or so.

other "boxers" I mentioned earlier will not also be about "dogs." I still might see a link to a page about George Foreman's dog, if he has one. But the hit list will be a lot closer to what I want.

If my hit list is still cluttered with the wrong kind of pages, I might remember that a Boxer is a breed of dog, so a page about Boxer dogs probably also uses the term "breed" prominently. So I might try a third term to further narrow the hit list: *Boxer dog breed*. Get the idea?

If you get too specific, you may accidentally omit a few pages you want. There may be Boxer dog pages that don't use "breed" anywhere that would show up in a search database. So it's best to start off with a happy medium (a term that's specific but not overly restrictive), see what you get, and then try subsequent searches using more or less specific terms, depending on what's in the hit list.

Using Operators to Control Searches

Whenever you use multiple words, you're using *operators*, even if you don't know it.

In mathematics, an operator is a word or symbol used to specify the action in an equation, such as plus or minus. Operators are used in search terms to express a logical equation of sorts that tightly controls how a search engine handle's the term.

Three basic operators are used in searching:

Using operators in this way is sometimes described as Boolean logic.

- **And.** When you use "and" between words in a search term, you tell the search engine to find only those pages that contain both of the words—pages that contain only one or the other are not included in the hit list.

- **Or.** When you use "or" between words in a search term, you tell the search engine to find all pages that contain either of the words—all pages that contain either word alone, or both words, are included in the hit list.

- **Not.** When you use "not" between words in a search term, you tell the search engine to find all pages that contain the word before not, then to remove from the hit list any that also contain the word following not.

The following table illustrates how operators affect the search results:

How Operators Work in Search Terms

Search Term	What a Search Tool Matches
Dodge and pickup	Only pages containing both "Dodge" and "pickup"
Dodge or pickup	All pages containing either "Dodge" or "pickup," or both words
Dodge not pickup	All pages that contain "Dodge" but do not also contain "pickup" (gets all the Dodge pages, then eliminates any about pickups)
Dodge and pickup and models	Pages that contain all three words
Dodge or pickup or models	Pages that contain any of the three words
Dodge not Chrysler	Pages that contain "Dodge" but do not also contain "Chrysler" (gets all the Dodge pages, then eliminates any that also mention Chrysler)

Before using operators in search terms, check out the options or instructions area of the search tool you intend to use. On the main page of most search tools, you can find a link leading to instructions.

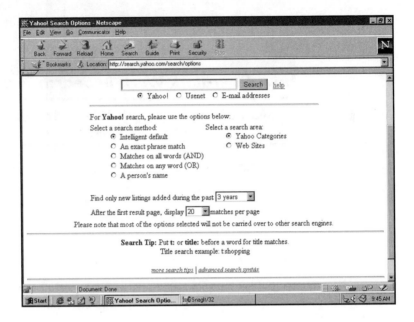

Most search tools support *and, or,* and *not,* but some have their
own little quirks about how you must go about it. For example,
Excite and Alta Vista prefer that you insert a plus sign (+) at the
beginning of a word rather than precede it with *and.*

PART

5

Finding Other Stuff

Most Internet searches seek Web pages—after all, that's where the action is. But did you know that you can use the Internet to find other stuff, such as programs and files for downloading, and the phone numbers or email addresses of friends and colleagues? This part shows you how by exploring these topics:

- About Files and Programs You Can Find
- Finding Programs and Files
- Finding Phone Numbers and Email Addresses

Cheat Sheet

What's Downloading, Anyhow?

Downloading is copying a computer file from a server, through the Net, to your computer so you can use it there. You locate a link that points to a file or program you want, then you download that file by clicking the link and following any prompts that appear.

How Long Does Downloading Take?

The larger the file, the longer it takes to download. Over a connection of 28.8Kbps, a 1MB file typically downloads in around 10 minutes. Download time can be unpredictable, however, because download speed is affected by many different factors, such as the current workload of the server from which you're downloading.

Choosing Files You Can Use

Not every file or program you find online works on every type of computer. You must make sure that the ones you download are compatible with your computer type, and often also with your operating system. You can often tell a file's system requirements by its filename extension, the final part of the filename that follows the period.

Keep the following points in mind as well:

- Usually, programs written just for DOS or Windows 3.1 also run in Windows 95, 98, or NT, although the reverse is never true.
- Almost any Windows 95 program runs in Windows 98 or NT, but some NT programs can't run in Windows 95 or Windows 98.
- A program always runs best on the system for which it was written.

17

About Files and Programs You Can Find

The group of people who use the Internet have only one thing universally in common: They all use a computer. So it's no surprise that computer programs and files are the most common "things" you can acquire through the Internet. You can find all kinds of Internet software, other kinds of programs (like games or word processors), documents (such as books or articles), and other useful files such as utilities and plug-ins online.

Basic Survival

What's Downloading, Anyway?

After you find a file or program, you can get it by *downloading* it. So here's a good place to learn exactly what downloading means.

Downloading is the act of copying a computer file from a server, through the Net to your computer so you can use it there, just as if you had installed it from a disk or CD-ROM.

Whether you've thought about it or not, when you're on the Web, you're really downloading all the time. For example, every time you open a Web page, the files that make up that page are temporarily copied from the server to your computer.

But here we're talking more deliberate downloading: You locate a link in a Web page that points to a file or program you want, then you download that file by clicking the link and following any prompts that appear. It's really that simple.

Many files online are ZIP files, using the extension .zip. You learn about ZIP files in Chapter 18, "Finding Programs and Files."

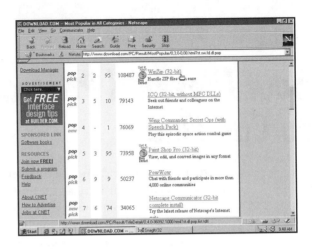

How Long Does Download-ing Take?

File size is expressed in kilobytes (K or KB) for smaller files, or in megabytes (M or MB) for larger files. 1MB = 1,024KB.

The larger the file, the longer it takes to download. That's why the size of the file is often shown somewhere in or near the link for downloading it.

How long does it take to download a file of a given size? That depends on many factors, including the speed of your Internet connection, and how busy the server is. But over a connection of 28.8Kbps, a 1MB file typically downloads in around 10 minutes, give or take a few. Over a 56Kbps connection, the same file downloads in a little over half that time.

You'll find a lot of great stuff to download that is less than 1MB in size. However, many programs or multimedia files can be much, much larger. A download of the entire Internet Explorer 4 program from Microsoft's Web site takes several hours, even through a 56Kbps connection.

With experience, you'll develop a sense of how long download-ing a file of a given size takes on your system. After you have that sense, always carefully consider the size of the file, and whether you want to wait that long for it, before starting the download.

Practice Download-ing a File

Just for practice, and to understand what to do after you locate a file you want, download the Adobe Acrobat reader, a program that enables you to display documents in the Adobe Acrobat (.pdf) file format, which are common online.

If you already
have an Adobe
Acrobat read-
er, or just
don't want
one, you can
cancel the
download
before it
finishes.

1. Go to Adobe's Web site at: www.adobe.com.

2. Locate and click the link or button labeled "Get Acrobat Reader" (or something similar).

3. Scroll down to the form for choosing a system type, and choose yours.

4. Near the bottom of the page, click the button labeled Download to submit the form. A page of instructions and links appears, containing information specific to the Adobe Acrobat Reader version for your system.

   You'll probably find two or more links for downloading the file, each next to the name of a city or country. Popular files are usually available from multiple servers, spread across the continent or globe. Choose the one closest to you.

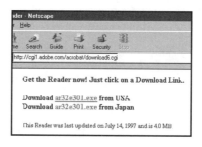

5. Click one of the links to the file.

   After you click the link, one or more dialog boxes appear prompting you to make a few easy choices regarding the file you're downloading.

   The exact dialog boxes you'll see differ by browser and computer type, but typically, a dialog box opens to ask whether you want to just save the file to disk after down-loading, or immediately open or run the file automatically.

You can
download
from any
server
shown, no
matter
where it is,
but always
try the one
closest to you
first.

147

When a link downloads a media file, such as a sound clip, your browser may open the file automatically after downloading.

6. After you deal with any dialog boxes that appear, the download begins, and a status message appears in a dialog box or in the Status bar at the bottom of the browser window, informing you of the download's progress.

In the download status message, some browsers also display an estimate of how much longer the download will take to finish. Although that estimate can be handy, it's just a guess, and should not be taken as an exact prediction of how long the download will take.

When the download is complete, the status message disappears. You may continue browsing, or go use the file you just downloaded.

The status message usually features a Cancel button, so you can quit the download before it finishes, if you want to.

Throughout a download, a status message appears to track its progress.

Beyond Survival

Choosing Files You Can Use

You can download any type of computer file, but not every file or program you find online works on every type of computer.

"Duh!", you may think. But you'd be surprised how often people forget this. Web browsing enables different kinds of computers to all look at the same online content, so after a while people tend to forget that off the Web, PCs, Macs, and other types of computers each use different kinds of files and programs.

When you search for files and programs, make sure the items you choose are compatible with your computer type and with your operating system (Windows 3.1, Windows 95, DOS, Mac OS 7 or OS 8, UNIX flavor, and so on).

The Two File Types: Program and Data

Although there are dozens of different types of files, they all generally fall into either of two groups:

- Program files. A program file contains a program—a game, a word processor, a plug-in, a utility, and so on. Program files are almost always designed to run on only one type of computer and operating system. For example, a program file designed for a Mac typically will not run in Windows. However, many programs are available in similar but separate versions, one for each system type.

Program files for Windows 95 almost always run on Windows 98, too.

- Data files. A data file contains information that can be displayed, or used in some other way, by a program. For example, a word processing document is a data file, to be displayed by a word processing program. Like program files, some data files can be used only by a particular program running on a particular computer type. But many data file types can be used on a variety of systems.

Common Data File Types on the Net

When you encounter a link to a file, you'll usually have no trouble telling what system the file is made for.

Often, before arriving at the link, you will have navigated through a series of links or form selections in which you specified your system type, so when you finally see links to files, they all point to files that can run on your system. In other cases, the link itself—or text near the link—tells you the system requirements for the file.

But even when the link doesn't fill you in, you can often tell a file's system requirements by its filename extension, the final part of the filename that follows the period. (For example, in the filename Monty.doc, the extension is .doc.)

The following table shows many of the most common file types online.

File Types You'll Find Online for Downloading

Extension	Type of File	Requirements
.exe, .com	Program file (a game,utility, application, and so on)	Runs on one (and only one) type of system. Always read any text near the link to be sure that a particular .exe or .com file will run on your computer.
.doc	Word document	Can be opened and edited in either the Windows or Mac version of Word, or Windows 95's WordPad program, and also can be displayed by Internet Explorer 4, or by Navigator if it is equipped with the ActiveX plug-in.
.pdf	Adobe Acrobat document	Can be opened in the Adobe Acrobat Reader program

Extension	Type of File	Requirements
		(available for a variety of systems) or in a browser equipped with an Adobe Acrobat plug-in. Can also be converted and displayed by some word processing programs.
.xls	Excel spreadsheet	Can be opened and edited in either the Windows or Mac version of Excel, and displayed by Internet Explorer 4, or by Navigator if it is equipped with the ActiveX plug-in.
.txt, .asc	Plain text file	Can be opened in any word processor or text editor on any system, and displayed by any browser.
.wri	Windows Write document	Can be displayed by Windows Write (in Windows 3.1) or WordPad (in Windows 95/98/NT).

continues

151

Continued

Extension	Type of File	Requirements
.avi, .mov, .qt, .mpg, .au, .mid, .snd	Various types of media files	Can be run by various player programs, or by your browser if it is equipped for them.
.zip	*Archive* containing one or more compressed files	Must be decompressed (*unzipped*) before the files it contains can be used; see Chapter 18.

PC Files Versus Mac Files

Few program files are designed to run on both Macs and PCs. However, if you use a PC, you should know that some programs work in multiple PC operating systems. For example, some programs are written to run in both Windows 3.1 and Windows 95, and sometimes DOS, as well.

Keep the following tips in mind when choosing file types:

- Programs written just for DOS or Windows 3.1 will usually also run in Windows 95, 98, or NT, although the reverse is never true.

- Almost any Windows 95 program will run in Windows 98 or NT, but some Windows NT programs will not run in Windows 95 or 98.

- Even with all this cross-system compatibility, a program always runs best on the system for which it was written, so favor choices that match what you have. For example, if you use Windows 95, and you're given a choice between Windows 3.1 and Windows 95 versions of a file, download the Windows 95 version.

- Even if you have a PowerPC-based Mac (which can optionally run some Windows programs), always favor true Mac files over PC versions, when you have a choice.

Cheat Sheet

Finding Sources for Programs and Files

Sites for finding and downloading software appear all over the Web. Many popular shareware programs have their own Web sites, and links to shareware products may be found on thousands of pages.

When you're looking for a shareware, freeware, or demo program to do a particular job, you'll have better luck if you visit a Web site designed to provide access to a wide range of products, sites such as

- shareware.com
- download.com

Using Commercial Software Sites

Frequent the Web sites of any commercial software companies whose products you use regularly. You can learn about new and enhanced versions of products you use, and also pick up tips, free enhancements, product support, and fixes for common problems.

Microsoft and Apple offer so many downloads that each provides its own search tools and directories for locating files:

- For Apple files, it's support.info.apple.com/ftp/swhome.html.
- For Microsoft files, it's www.microsoft.com/msdownload/.

Working with ZIP Files

Some files online are *compressed*—converted into smaller files—to cut the download time. After downloading, you must decompress a compressed file to restore it to its original size and use it. A utility program such as WinZip is required to decompress or "unzip" these files so you can use them.

18

Finding Programs and Files

To find a particular file or program you want, you can apply
the search techniques you've already picked up in Part 4,
"Finding Web Sites." But in this chapter, you'll learn search
techniques that are better focused so you can find the exact files
you want.

Basic Survival

**Finding
Sources for
Programs
and Files**

Where you begin looking for a file depends on the how that file
is offered on the Web, or rather, in what way that file is licensed
for use by those other than its creator. Most software falls into
one of the following four groups:

- Commercial. The programs you can buy in a box at the
software store. Many software companies have Web sites,
where you can learn about their products and often
download them as well. Typically, you fill in an online
form to pay for the software, then download it.

- Demo. Demo software is commercial software that has
some features disabled, or automatically stops working—
expires—after you use it for a set number of days. Demo
software is distributed free on commercial and shareware
sites, and provides a free preview of the real thing.

- Shareware. Shareware is software you're allowed to try out
for free, but for which you are supposed to pay. After the
trial period (usually 30 days), you either pay the programmer or stop using the program. Some shareware
expires or has features disabled, like demo software, so
you won't continue using it without paying.

- Freeware. Freeware is free software you may use all you
want, as long as you want, for free.

Appendix B
shows the
URLs of a
great selection
of sites for
getting share-
ware, free-
ware, and
commercial
software.

All-Purpose Shareware Sites

Sites for downloading shareware appear all over the Web. Many popular shareware programs have their own Web sites, and links to shareware products may be found on thousands of pages, such as Yahoo!'s shareware directory at

www.yahoo.com/Computers_and_Internet/Software/Shareware/

But when you're looking for a shareware, freeware, or demo program to do a particular job, you'll have better luck if you visit a Web site designed to provide access to a wide range of products, sites such as

- Shareware.com. Whose easy-to-remember URL is shareware.com.

- Download.com. (Can you guess the URL?)

These sites are very much like the search tools you used in Part 4, providing search term boxes, directories, and other tools for finding files. But the hits they produce are always either links to files that match your search, or links to other Web pages from which those files may be downloaded.

Sites like Shareware.com don't store the files themselves; they just provide links that lead to files stored on other servers.

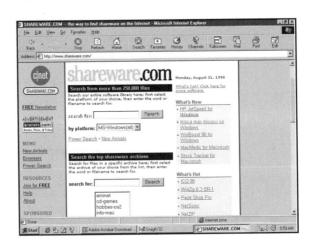

The key to using Shareware.com, Download.com, and similar file-finders is to make sure that your search specifies both of the following:

- The kind of file or program you seek: email, word processing, game, paint program—whatever you want.

- Your computer type and operating system: Windows 95, Mac OS8, and so on.

If you include this information in your search, the hit list shows only files and programs of the kind you want, and only those that run on your particular system.

Finding a Program on Shareware. com

For practice, try finding a solitaire game for your system at Shareware.com:

1. Go to Shareware.com at `shareware.com`.

2. In the box labeled Quick Search, type `solitaire`.

3. From the list below the Quick Search box, select your system type.

4. Click the button labeled Search. After a few moments, a hit list of solitaire games for your system appears.

5. Choose a file link, and click it. Depending on the file, the download may commence, or a new list of links appears, each pointing to the identical file stored on a different server. Click one to start the download.

Each hit shows a link to the file, the file size and type, and a brief description of the file's contents.

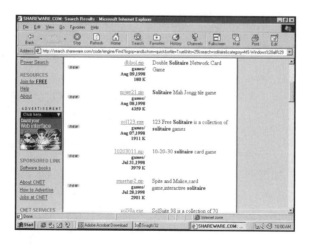

A Windows Search Tip

If you use Windows 95 or 98, and a search for Windows 95/98 programs doesn't get you what you want, try another search for any Windows file of the type you want. For example, in Shareware.com, you'd choose MS-Windows (all) from the list of system types.

Such a search turns up both Windows 95 and Windows 3.1 hits. You can substitute a Windows 3.1 program when no Windows 95 program is available.

Beyond Survival

Using Commercial Software Sites

As a Web user, you have a lot to gain by frequenting the Web sites of any commercial software companies whose products you use regularly. You can learn about new and enhanced versions of products you use, and also pick up tips, free enhancements, product support, and fixes for common problems.

In particular, it's important to know about the Web site of the maker of the operating system you use on your computer: Microsoft's site (for Windows users) and Apple's (for Mac OS folks). On these sites, you can find all sorts of free updates and utilities for your operating system, fixes for problems, utilities, and news about upcoming new releases and enhancements.

Microsoft and Apple offer so many downloads that each provides its own search tools and directories for locating the file you need. The best place to start:

- For Apple files, `support.info.apple.com/ftp/swhome.html`.

- For Microsoft files, `www.microsoft.com/msdownload/`.

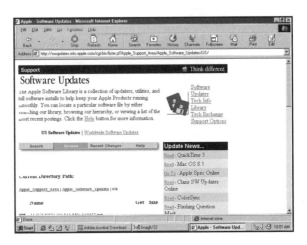

Working with ZIP Files

The larger a file is, the longer it takes to download. So some files online are compressed—converted into smaller files—to cut the download time. After downloading, you must decompress a compressed file to restore it to its original size and use it.

Also, most application programs are made up not just of one fat file, but of a collection of program and data files. A single compressed file can pack together many separate files, so they can all be downloaded together in one step.

A compressed file containing multiple files is sometimes called an archive.

There are several forms of compression used online, but by far the most popular form is called ZIP. A ZIP file uses the extension .zip and must be decompressed—*unzipped*—after downloading before you can use the file or files it contains.

You need a special program to unzip ZIP files. If you don't already have one, the most popular shareware unzippers are:

- For Windows, WinZIP, which you can download from www.winzip.com.

- For Mac, ZipIt, which you can download from www.awa.com/softlock/zipit/zipit.html.

After installing an unzipping program, you can decompress any ZIP file by opening the program, choosing the ZIP file you want to decompress and then choosing Extract from a toolbar or menu.

159

ZIP Files That Aren't ZIP Files

You usually open a self-extracting archive just by double-clicking its file icon.

One special type of .exe program file is called a *self-extracting archive*, which is a compressed file or files, just like a ZIP file.

Unlike a ZIP file, however, a self-extracting archive file does not require an unzipping program. Instead, it decompresses itself automatically when you open it. Most large applications offered online, such as Web browsers, download as self-extracting archives.

Cheat Sheet

Using People-Finding Sites

You use people-searching tools like any other search tool: Enter as much as you know about the person and the tool finds matches in its database. Some people finders are

- Yahoo!'s People Search, at `people.yahoo.com`.
- Excite's US People Finder, at `www.excite.com/Reference/people.html`.

Search-Success Tips

When the SmartNames check box is checked, Yahoo!'s people finder searches not only for the exact first name you supplied, but also for common variations of that name.

In Yahoo!'s Advanced Email search, a Flexible Search check box also appears, in which you need enter only the first part of a name, if you're unsure about its correct ending.

Using People Finders Through Your Email Program

Searching an LDAP directory from within your email program is just like using a people finder on the Web: You fill in a name and other information in a form. But instead of starting on a Web page, you go online, open your email program, and navigate to the LDAP search:

- In Netscape Messenger, choose Communicator, Address Book, and then click the Directory button in the Address Book's toolbar.
- In Internet Explorer's Outlook Express, click the Address Book button on the toolbar, and then click the Find button in the Address Book's toolbar.

Other Folk-Finding Tips

- Use a company or school directory.
- Try name variations.
- Use an online service directory.

19

Finding Phone Numbers and Email Addresses

Using the search techniques much like those you've picked up in the preceding three chapters, you can find people on the Internet, or rather, the email addresses, mailing addresses, or telephone numbers through which particular people may be reached.

Basic Survival

Using People-Finding Sites

As with all types of search tools, every people finder on the Web draws from a different database of names and contact information.

For any particular name, a search using one tool may turn up no hits, although a search with a different tool may hit pay dirt. It's important to know where several different search tools are, so if one tool fails, you can try another.

You use most people-searching tools like any other search tool: Enter as much as you know about the person—name, city, and so on—and the tool finds matches in its database.

Some of the better people finders are:

- Yahoo!'s People Search, at `www.yahoo.com/search/people/`
- Excite's US People Finder (for addresses and phone numbers), at `www.excite.com/Reference/people.html`
- Excite's Email Lookup (for email addresses), at `www.excite.com/reference/email_lookup`
- Bigfoot, at `www.Bigfoot.com`
- Four11, at `www.Four11.com`

Fourll = "411"—directory assistance. Get it?

When considering a people search, keep the following points in mind:

- If the person you seek may have his or her own Web page, using a people-finding tool may not be necessary. Instead, perform an ordinary Web search with a tool like Alta Vista or Excite, using the person's name as your search term (see Chapter 16, "Using Search Terms"). Such a search may turn up that person's home page, on which you'll probably find contact information.

- Depending on the people finder you use and the options you choose, you may find a person's mailing address, phone number, or email address (or all three). Of course, you haven't learned how to use email yet, but that's okay—you'll learn all about it in Part 6, "Exchanging Email." For now, if a search turns up an email address, just jot it down and save it for Part 6.

Find Yourself

Because you're probably already familiar with Yahoo!, Yahoo!'s People Search is a great first place to try finding someone. Practice by finding yourself:

1. Go to Yahoo!'s People Search at `people.yahoo.com`.

You can also reach the People Search by going to www.yahoo.com and then clicking the People Search link near the top.

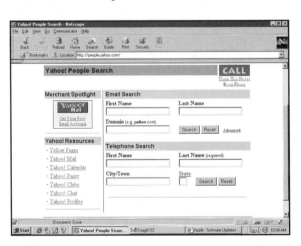

2. Complete the boxes in the Telephone Search form: First Name, Last Name, City, State.

You can skip any boxes you're not sure about, but you must at least enter a last name and state.

3. Click the button labeled Search that appears directly to the right of the Telephone Search form. After a few moments, any matches appear in a hit list.

4. Click Back to return to the People Search. This time, fill in the boxes under Email Search, and click the Search button to the right of the Email Search form. Did your email address appear?

5. Just for fun, try another Telephone or Email Search, but this time, leave some boxes empty. For example, fill in your name, but not your city or state. The hit list will show others, all over the United States, who have the same name as you.

6. Finally, click the Advanced link next to the Email Search and Reset buttons. A new form appears on which you can supply more detailed information for performing an advanced search for someone's email address.

How Do the People Finders Get My Number?

By agreeing to have your number listed in the phone book, you've agreed to make it public—it will wind up online.

If you found yourself in your Yahoo! searches, you may be wondering, "How did my phone number, email address, or other information get on the Web?"

Most information in the search tool databases—including names, addresses, and phone numbers—comes from public telephone records. Some databases may also obtain records from other online databases (such as your ISP's user directory, for email addresses), or even from online forms you've submitted from Web pages.

So even if you have an unlisted telephone number (which phone companies call "unpublished"), a record about you may find its way into a database from another source. That's just one reason you must be careful about how and when you enter information about yourself in an online form (see Chapter 10, "Protecting Your Privacy").

Search Success Tips

Observe that Yahoo!'s people finder includes a check box for SmartNames.

When this check box is checked, Yahoo! searches not only for the exact first name you supplied, but also for common variations of that name. If you entered "Edward," the search might match records for "Edward," "Ed," "Eddy," and maybe "Ted." This increases the chances of finding the right person when you're not sure which name form the person uses.

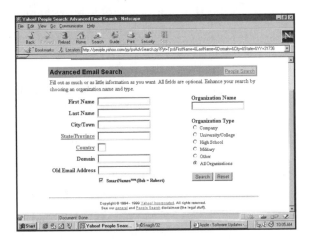

Beyond Survival

Using People Finders Through Your Email Program

A family of people-finding directories, known collectively as LDAP directories, exists specifically and solely for finding email addresses, both in North America and worldwide.

Some LDAP directories, such as the aforementioned Bigfoot (www.Bigfoot.com) and Four11 (www.Four11.com) are accessible through a Web page. But these and several other LDAPs may also be accessed from within some email programs. This enables you to search for an email address from within your email program—which is, after all, the place you need email addresses.

LDAP means Lightweight Directory Access Protocol, but you really don't need to remember that.

You won't meet email until Part 6, but this is a good place to show how an email program can be a people finder.

The email programs included in the big two Internet Suites both support LDAP searches from within their Address Book, a utility that helps you keep track of email addresses.

Searching an LDAP directory from within your email program is just like using a people finder on the Web: You fill in a name and other information in a form. The only difference is getting to that form. Instead of opening a Web page, you go online, open your email program, and navigate to the LDAP search form as follows:

- In Netscape's Messenger program, choose Communicator, Address Book to open the Address Book, then click the Directory button in the Address Book's toolbar. A search dialog box opens. Use the top list in the dialog box to choose the LDAP directory to search, fill in the other boxes, and click Search.

- In Internet Explorer's Outlook Express program, click the Address Book button on the toolbar to open the Address Book, then click the Find button in the Address Book's toolbar. A search dialog box opens. Use the top list in the dialog box to choose the LDAP directory to search, fill in the other boxes, and click Find Now.

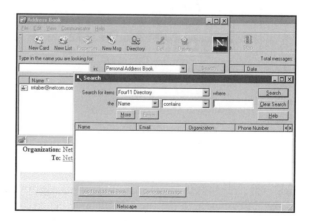

Other Folk-Finding Tips

The all-around easiest ways to find people online are those I've already described. But if those don't pay off for you, try the ideas in the following paragraphs.

Use a company or school directory. Do you know the name of the company the person works for, or a school he or she attends? Many companies, colleges, and universities have their own Web sites, and those Web sites often contain employee and student directories you can browse or search. Just search for and go to the Web site, then browse for a link to a directory.

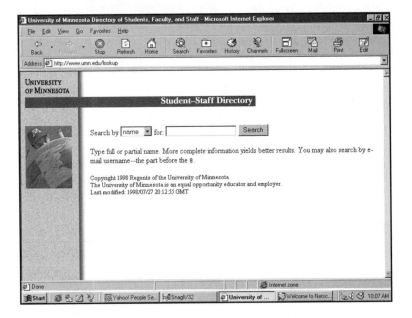

Try name variations. Might the person you're looking for sometimes use a different name than the one you've been using as a search term? Try alternate spellings (Sandy, Sandi) or nicknames. Try both the married name and birth name of people who may have married or divorced recently.

You may also want to try a compound name made out of both the birth name and married name (Jacqueline Bouvier Kennedy); I know both men and women who use compound or hyphenated married names.

Only the online service's customers can access its user directory.

Use an online service directory. If you use an online service (such as America Online) and think the person you seek may use the same online service you do, try your online service's own directory of its users. You can access the directory from within the service's interface for non-Internet content.

PART

6

Exchanging Email

Web browsing is the hottest Internet activity, but email is probably the most widely used and most productive one.

Using Internet email—which has become such an everyday fixture that many people now call it plain "mail"—you can easily exchange messages with anyone else on the Internet. An email message typically reaches its addressee within minutes (or at most, an hour or so), even on the opposite side of the globe. It's faster than paper mail, easier than faxing, and sometimes just plain fun.

In this part, you explore

- Getting Started with Email
- Composing and Sending Email
- Receiving Email from Others
- Stopping Junk Email

Cheat Sheet

Understanding Email Addresses

To send someone email, you need his or her email address. An email address always has that "at" symbol (@) in the middle of it.

Setting Up Your Email Program

Internet suites such as Internet Explorer 4 and Netscape Communicator include an email client. In the suites, the programs are called

- Messenger, in Netscape Communicator
- Outlook Express, in Internet Explorer 4

Getting Around in Your Email Program

Messenger and Outlook Express divide their messaging activities into a family of folders, including Inbox (new messages).

Displaying a Message

From the list displayed by each folder, you can display any message:

- Single-click the message in the list to display it in the preview pane in the bottom of the window.
- Double-click the message in the list to display it in its own message window.

20

Getting Started with Email

Before you begin composing, sending, and receiving email, it's important to learn a little bit about email addresses, programs, and more.

Basic Survival

Understanding Email Addresses

To send email to someone, all you need is that person's Internet email address. An email address is easy to spot: It always has the "at" symbol (@) in the middle of it. For example, you know at a glance that

    sammy@fishbait.com

is an email address. In most email addresses, everything following the @ symbol is the server address of a company, Internet service provider (ISP), or other organization. The part before the @ is the name (or user ID) of a particular employee or user. For example, the addresses

    SallyP@genco.com

    mikey@genco.com

    Manager_of_Sales@genco.com

obviously belong to three different people, all of whom work for the same company or use the same ISP (whatever Genco is).

Each online service has its own mail server address, too: For example, America Online's is `aol.com` and Microsoft Network's is `msn.com`. You can tell that the email address

    neddyboy@aol.com

is that of an America Online user named "neddyboy."

Setting Up Your Email Program

There are many different email programs out there.

Internet suites such as Internet Explorer 4 and Netscape Communicator include an email client—but you must take care when installing these programs not to optionally omit the email component of the suite. Choosing the "full" installation option when setting up a suite ensures that you include all the suite's client programs.

If you don't use a suite, see the "Beyond Survival" section to learn about getting an email program.

In the suites, the programs are called:

- Messenger (or Messenger Mailbox, in some versions), in Netscape Communicator. You can open Messenger from within the Navigator browser by choosing Communicator, Messenger.

- Outlook Express, in Internet Explorer 4. You can open Outlook Express from within the Internet Explorer browser by choosing Go, Mail.

You can also open Outlook Express by clicking the Start menu and choosing Programs, Internet Explorer, Outlook Express.

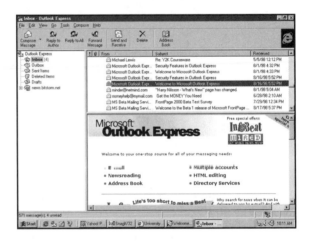

Configuring Email

After installing an email program, you need to configure it before you can use it. All email programs have a configuration dialog box of some kind (or a series of dialog boxes) on which you can enter the information required for exchanging email.

You'll find the configuration dialog boxes:

You can use a wizard to automatically configure Outlook Express while setting up your Internet connection.

- In Messenger, by choosing Edit, Preferences to open the Preferences dialog box. In the Category list, choose Mail & Groups. Complete the configuration settings in the Mail & Groups category's Identity and Mail Server subcategories.

- In Outlook Express, by completing the Mail dialog boxes of the Connection Wizard. If you open Outlook Express without having configured it first, the Connection Wizard opens automatically.

Open the suites' email programs without first configuring, and a dialog box opens to prompt for configuration information.

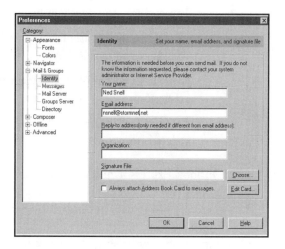

The configuration dialog boxes for most email programs require most or all of the following information (all of which your Internet provider will tell you):

- Your full name.

You don't need your ISP to tell you your name—do you?

- Your full email address. Some configuration dialog boxes make you indicate the two parts of your address separately: the *username*—the part of the email address preceding the @ symbol—and your *domain*—the part of the email address following the @ symbol.

- The address of your ISP's outgoing mail server, sometimes called SMTP.

- The address of your ISP's incoming mail server, sometimes called POP3.

Also, to ensure that no one but you gets your email, most ISPs require you to choose and use an email password. Some email programs let you enter that password in the configuration dialog box, so you needn't type a password each time you check your email.

Getting Around in Your Email Program

Messenger and Outlook Express divide their messaging activities into a family of folders. In each folder, you see a list of messages you can display or work with in other ways. The folders are

- Inbox. Lists messages you have received.

- Outbox (called Unsent Messages in Messenger). Lists messages you have composed but saved to be sent later.

- Sent. Lists copies of all messages you've sent, for your reference.

- Deleted (called Trash in Messenger). Lists messages you've deleted from any other folder.

Outlook Express handles two different jobs: email and newsgroups (see Chapter 25, "Observing Proper Netiquette"). It therefore has folders not only for email, but also for newsgroups. Before performing an email activity in Outlook Express, always be sure that you're in an email-related folder, such as Inbox or Outbox, and not the News folder.

To switch among folders:

- In Messenger, choose a folder from the drop-down list that appears just below the toolbar.

- In Outlook Express, click a folder name in the panel along the left side of the window.

Displaying a Message

From the list displayed by each folder, you can display any message. You do this in either of two ways (the steps are the same in both Outlook Express and Messenger):

- Single-click the message in the list to display it in the preview pane in the bottom of the window.

- Double-click the message in the list to display it in its own message window.

Preview Pane

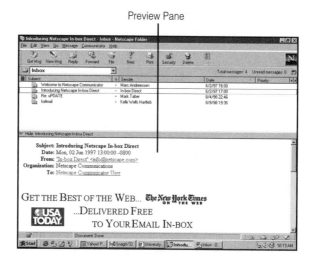

Message Window

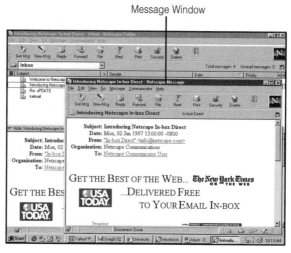

177

The preview pane is best to use when you're scanning messages, and need to move quickly from one to the next. Use a full message window to read a long message or to read a message you will reply to or forward (as described in Chapter 22, "Receiving Email from Others").

Beyond Survival

Finding an Email Client

If you don't already have an email client, you may apply the file-finding techniques from Part 5, "Finding Other Stuff," to search for one. Another good source for email and other Internet clients is the Tucows directory at

    tucows.mcp.com

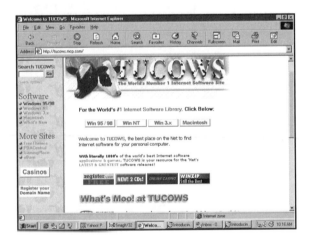

Among the links you'll likely find in any search for email programs are links to various versions of a program called Eudora, one of the most popular email clients outside of the suites.

If you want to go straight to learning about and downloading Eudora (which is available for both Mac and Windows in a freeware version called Eudora Light and a commercial version, Eudora Pro), visit the site of Eudora's maker at

    www.eudora.com

Using AutoConnect

When working with email, the only time you need to be connected to the Internet is at the moments when you actually *send* messages—transmit them to the Internet (see Chapter 21, "Composing and Sending Email")—or receive messages—copy them from the Internet to your computer (see Chapter 22). You can be online or offline while composing messages, reading messages you've received, or managing your messages.

Because of this, many email programs are integrated with the "auto-connect" capabilities built in to systems such as Mac OS8 or Windows 95. When your system's auto-connect feature is enabled, the email program attempts to connect you automatically to the Internet when necessary.

For example, if you've composed a message offline, when you attempt to send it, your Internet connection dialog box may open, prompting you to go online so the message can be sent.

If you can't auto-connect, just connect to the Internet before sending or receiving email, but remember that you can read or write email offline.

Cheat Sheet

Writing Your Message

To compose a message, open a new message window:

- In Messenger, click the New Msg button on the toolbar.
- In Outlook Express, click the Compose Message toolbar button.

Type the recipient's email address in the To line, type a subject in the Subject line, and then type the message in the large body area.

Sending a Message Now

Send the message by clicking the Send button in the toolbar.

Sending a Message Later

To save a message for sending later:

- In Messenger, choose File, Send Later.
- In Outlook Express, first check that you're in offline mode by choosing File and looking for a check mark next to Work Offline in the File menu. Then return to the message and click Send.

To send all messages that are waiting:

- In Messenger, choose File, Send Unsent Messages.
- In Outlook Express, click the Send and Receive button.

Sending One Message to Several People at Once

You can send a message to multiple recipients in several ways: entering multiple addresses (separated by semicolons) in the To line, entering other recipients in the Cc or Bcc lines, and sending to a mailing list created in the address book.

Using an Address Book

To create address book entries:

- In Outlook Express, choose Tools, Address Book, New Contact.
- In Messenger, choose Communicator, Address Book, New Card.

21

Composing and Sending Email

After you have something to say, and the address of someone to whom you want to say it, you're ready to start sending email.

Basic Survival

Writing Your Message

In most email programs, you compose your message in a window that's much like a word processing program, with a special form at the top for filling in the address and subject information—the message's header. Below the form for the header, you type your message text in the large space provided for the message body.

To compose a message:

1. Open a new message window, in which you can compose a message. You do this from any email-related folder, such as Inbox.

In Messenger, click the New Msg button on the toolbar.

In Outlook Express, click the Compose Message button on the toolbar.

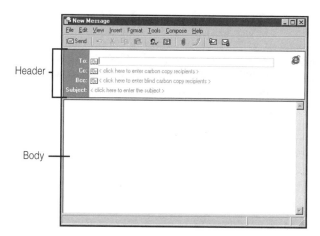

2. Click in the To line (in the header, near the top of the window), and type the email address of the person to whom you want to send a message.

3. Click in the Subject line, and type a concise, meaningful subject for your message.

4. Click in the large panel of the new message window and type your message, just as you would in a word processor.

The subject you type appears in the message list of the recipient, to explain the mail's purpose.

As a rule, you cannot use text formatting (fonts, bold, italic, underlining, and so on) in an email message, so for now, stick to simple text. In Chapter 40, "Creating Fancy, Formatted Messages," you learn how to do some fancy message formatting. Note, however, that many email recipients cannot display such messages.

Sending a Message Now

After the header and body of the message are complete, you send your message on its way. In most programs, you send by clicking a button labeled Send and Receive 📧 in the toolbar of the window in which you composed the message.

The message is immediately sent to your ISP's mail server, and from there it will be routed to its destination. If you composed the message offline, and your email program supports your computer's auto-connect feature (refer to Chapter 20, "Getting Started with Email"), you'll be automatically connected to the Net when you click Send.

Most programs have a "Sent" folder, in which a copy of every message you send is saved, for later reference.

Beyond Survival

Sending a Message Later

When you're composing several messages offline, as you complete each one you need not connect and send, disconnect, connect and send, disconnect, and so on.

Instead, as you complete each message, you can save it in your Outbox or Unsent Messages folder instead of sending it right away. You can then send all the waiting messages at once, the next time you connect.

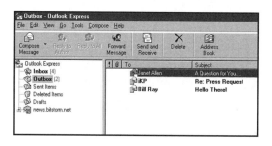

To save a message for sending later:

- In Messenger, save the message in your Unsent Messages folder by choosing File, Send Later instead of clicking the Send button.

When you send a message to the Outbox folder, a message appears to tell you that the message isn't being sent right away.

- In Outlook Express, first check that you're in offline mode by choosing File and looking for a check mark next to Work Offline in the File menu. (If you see no check mark, click the Work Offline item in the menu to put one there.) Then return to the message and click Send.

Messages in Outbox or Unsent Messages wait there, safe and sound, until you're ready to send them. You can even shut down your computer, and when you start up again, the messages will be there.

When you're ready to send all messages that are waiting:

- In Messenger, choose File, Send Unsent Messages.

- In Outlook Express, click the Send and Receive button on the toolbar (see Chapter 22, "Receiving Email from Others").

Sending One Message to Several People at Once

You can instantly send one message to many different people at once. This is a great way to conveniently make announcements or share information with a group.

There are four different ways to send a message to multiple recipients:

- In the To: line of the header, type all the email addresses. Type a semicolon (;) after each address except the final one.

- To "cc" (carbon copy) your email to recipients other than your primary addressee(s), click the Cc: line in the message header, and enter one or more email addresses there. (If you Cc: to more than one person, separate addresses with a semicolon.)

Bcc = a secret copy; when you send a Bcc, recipients in the To and Cc lines can't tell that you also sent to the people in Bcc.

- To "bcc" (blind carbon copy) your email to recipients other than your primary addressee(s), click the Bcc: line in the message header, and enter one or more email addresses there. (Separate multiple addresses with a semicolon.)

184

- Use your email program's address book (see the next section) to create a custom mailing list, then put the mailing list address in the message's To line.

Using an Address Book

Most folks find that there's a steady list of others to whom they email often. Keeping track of those all-important names and addresses, and using them, is easier when you use your email program's address book.

When an addressee's information is in your address book, you needn't type—or even remember—his or her email address. Instead, you can choose the person's name from the address book, and your email program fills in the address for you.

To create an address book entry:

- In Outlook Express, choose Tools, Address Book, New Contact.

- In Messenger, choose Communicator, Address Book, New Card.

Some address books use nicknames— short, easy-to-remember names you type in the To line instead of the full address.

Most stuff in a new entry is optional; only a name and email address are required.

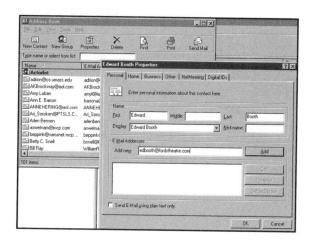

To use an address book entry to address a message, begin by opening the new message window as usual. Then open the address book list:

- In Messenger, click the Address button.

- In Outlook Express, click the little Rolodex card icon in the To line.

In the list, click the name of an addressee, and click the To button to add the addressee to the To line, or Cc to add the addressee to the Cc line.

When you are done choosing recipients, click OK to close the address book.

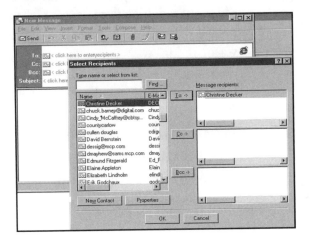

Cheat Sheet

Getting Your New Messages

To receive messages:

- In Messenger, click the Get Msg button on the toolbar.
- In Outlook Express, open any email-related folder (Inbox is a good choice) and click the Send and Receive button.

A dialog box may appear to prompt for your email password. Type your email password and press Enter to continue receiving email.

Replying to Messages

To reply, open the message to which you're replying in your email program. From the message window's toolbar, click :

- Reply to Author (or Reply to Sender) to reply to the person who sent you the message.
- Reply to All (or Reply to Sender and All Recipients) to reply to the person who sent you the message and to everyone else to whom the message was sent when it was sent to you.

To complete the reply, type your comments above, below, or within the quote, and then click Send.

Forwarding Messages

To forward a message to a third party, open the original message in your email program. From the message window's toolbar, click Forward.

Fill in the To line with the address of the person you're forwarding to, type your comments above, below, or within the quote, and then click Send.

22

Receiving Email from Others

Has someone sent you email yet? How would you know? Time to learn how to retrieve all the exciting new information coming your way in email messages.

Basic Survival

Getting Your New Messages

When others send messages to you, those messages go to your ISP's or online service's mail server and wait there until you choose to receive them—copy them from the server to your computer.

To receive messages:

- In Messenger, click the Get Msg button on the toolbar.

- In Outlook Express, open any email-related folder (Inbox is a good choice) and click the Send and Receive button on the toolbar.

Using Your Email Username and Password

When you signed up for your Internet account, your provider gave you an email username and password.

After you click the button to receive mail, a dialog box may appear to prompt for your email password. Just type your email password and press Enter to continue receiving email.

Depending on your provider, your email username and password may be the same as your Internet logon username and password.

Your mail program contacts your ISP and checks for any new messages addressed to you:

- If there are no new messages, the words "No new messages on server" appear in the status bar at the bottom of the window.

- If there are new messages, the messages are copied to your computer and stored in your Inbox folder, where you can read them any time, online or off.

In the message lists displayed by most email programs, the messages you have not yet read appear in bold.

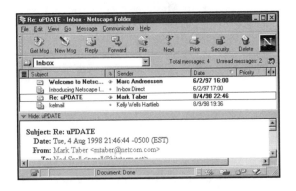

In the configuration dialog boxes of some email programs, you can type your email password. Then when you receive mail, the email program supplies the password for you, saving you a step. This feature is handy, but should be used only if your computer is located where no one else might try to retrieve and read your email if you strolled away from your desk while connected to the Internet.

Beyond Survival

Replying to Messages

The buttons shown are from Outlook Express; your buttons may differ.

Most email clients provide you with an easy way to create new messages by using messages you have received: *replying*.

To reply, you begin by opening the message to which you're replying in your email program. From the message window's toolbar, you then click a button like one of the following:

- Reply to Author  (or Reply to Sender). Creates a reply to the person who sent you the message.

- Reply to All (or Reply to Sender and All Recipients). Creates a reply to the person who sent you the message and to everyone else to whom the message was sent when it was sent to you. (Anyone in the original message's To: or Cc: lines will get your reply, but not any Bcc: recipients.)

Click Messenger's Reply button, and two choices appear: Reply to Sender and Reply to Sender and All Recipients.

Whichever button you click, a new message window opens. In the body of the message, a complete quote of the original message appears. A quote is all or a portion of a message you've received, included in a reply to indicate what you're replying to.

Click Messenger's Reply button, and two choices appear: Reply to Sender and Reply to Sender and All Recipients.

191

Cut from a quote the parts not relevant to your reply, and insert comments above, below, or within a quote.

Forwarding Messages

In the message window, the To line is automatically filled in for you, with the address of the person from whom you received the message (or multiple addresses, if you chose Reply to All). The Subject line is filled in with the original message's subject, preceded by Re: (regarding, or reply to), to indicate that your message is a reply to a message using that subject.

To complete the reply, all you have to do is type your comments above, below, or within the quote, and then click Send.

To forward a message you've received is to pass a copy of it to a third party. You might forward a message because you want to share the message's content with the third party, or because you believe that the third party is a more appropriate recipient for it than you.

As with a reply, you begin by opening the original message in your email program. From the message window's toolbar, you then click a Forward button [Forward].

A new message window opens. In the body of the message, a complete quote of the original message appears.

In the message window, the To line is empty, so you can enter the address of the person to whom you want to forward the message. (As with any message, you may enter multiple To recipients, and Cc recipients as well.) The Subject line is filled in with the original message's subject, preceded by FW: (forward).

To complete the forward, address the message, type your comments above, below, or within the quote, and then click Send.

Cheat Sheet

Spam-Preventive Surfing

The most important step in stopping spam is limiting the extent to which your address is known. To do that, limit the extent to which you

- Reveal your email address in online forms.
- Post to newsgroups.
- Accept cookies.
- Subscribe to mailing lists.

Curbing AOL Spam

If you use America Online, you may reduce spam by signing up for the Preferred Mail function (keyword PREFERRED MAIL).

Will a Furious Reply Stop a Spammer?

Angry replies never stop a spammer. Following "REMOVE" instructions you may see in a spam message can work, but such instructions may also be a trick that can expose you to even *more* spammage.

Filtering Out Spam

You can purchase utility programs designed to filter out spam:

- SpamNet at www.spamnet.com
- SpamKiller at novasoft.base.org
- eFilter at www.eflash.com
- SpamBlaster at www.gooware.com

Finding Filter Controls in Your Email Program

Most email programs have their own built-in filtering systems you can apply to control spam (to some extent):

- In Messenger, choose Edit, Mail Filters.
- In Outlook Express, choose Tools, Inbox Assistant.

23

Stopping Junk Email

Within a few weeks after you begin using the Internet, you'll make an unpleasant discovery: The same sort of take-no-prisoners direct marketing types who telemarket you at supper time and stuff offers in your mailbox have found you online.

Over time, you'll see an ever-increasing number of ads, offers, chain letters, pyramid schemes, scams, and general mischief arrive in your Inbox. This stuff—called *spam*—is a growing problem on the Net. Here's what you can do.

Basic Survival

Where Does Spam Come From?

Nothing can stop spam completely. But the methods in this chapter can help you minimize it.

Using variations on the same techniques you discovered in Chapter 21, "Composing and Sending Email," for sending a message to multiple recipients, anyone can automatically crank out an email ad to thousands—millions, even—of Internet users all at once.

Net veterans call these messages "spam" because they repeat and multiply the way the word spam does in a song from an old Monty Python skit.

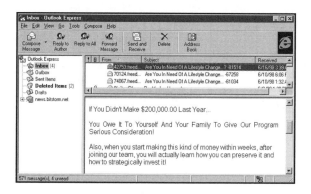

These messages often have subject lines designed to entice you into reading the message ("FREE $$$") or to trick you into doing so ("MESSAGE FROM AN OLD FRIEND"). As the Internet population has grown, so has the junk mail problem.

Spam-Preventive Surfing

The more widely known your email address is, the more spam you'll get—it's that simple. So the first and most important step in stopping spam is being very careful about how and when you reveal your email address.

To learn about efforts to outlaw spam, check out www.cauce.org

Unfortunately, it's hard to fully enjoy the Internet while keeping your email address a total secret. Many online activities, such as shopping (see Chapter 35, "Shopping Online") or posting to newsgroups (see Chapter 26, "Getting Started with Newsgroups"), create an online record of your email address. In fact, anytime you send email, an unscrupulous spammer may harvest your address by intercepting messages on their way across the Net.

Still, you can effectively limit the extent to which your address is known by making some smart surfing choices. In particular, be careful about the following:

- Be very careful how and when you fill out online forms or surveys (refer to Chapter 10, "Protecting Your Privacy"). A growing number of Web sites request that you complete a form to "register" to use the site; the form data is almost always used for marketing, and often for spam.

- On any site where you might complete a form, look for a link to a "Privacy Policy"; some Web sites promise in their policy not to spam you or to sell your information to spammers.

If you post to a sex-related newsgroup, you will receive spam pitching phone sex and other such products or services.

- When you post to a newsgroup, a spammer can easily learn two things about you: Your email address, and that you're interested in the newsgroup's topic.

- If you post a message on a newsgroup about a particular kind of product, you can expect to receive spam trying to sell you such a product. You can usually *read* newsgroup messages anonymously—but when you post, you reveal your address. So watch where you post.

- Cookies are files on your computer stored there by a Web site to record information about you that the page can access next time you visit. Unfortunately, the cookies on your computer—which may contain your email address and other personal data—may be read not only by the servers that put them there, but by other servers you visit, who may use that information for spam.

See Chapter 11 to learn more about cookies—including how to reject them, if you so choose.

- When you subscribe to mailing lists (see Chapter 24, "Subscribing to a Mailing List"), your name and email address (and implicitly, your interest in the list's topic) are recorded in a database that may be accessed and copied easily by a spammer, particularly if the list is managed by a program called a Listserv.

- A newsgroup covering the same topic that a mailing list covers is a safer choice, as long as you don't post to it. But if you intend to contribute to the discussion, the mailing list is still less spam-risky than the newsgroup.

Curbing AOL Spam

Stopping spam is a little trickier for users of online services than for users of ISPs. The online services derive some of their revenue from advertisers, for providing access to you. So they're not too keen on letting you block those ads.

If you use America Online, you can reduce spam by signing up for the Preferred Mail function (keyword PREFERRED MAIL), which blocks messages from many spammers.

Also, experts on AOL and spam advise users to avoid posting messages on AOL's forums and to use Internet newsgroups instead. Despite the spam exposure risk in newsgroups, AOL forums are notoriously harvested by spammers.

Will a Furious Reply Stop a Spammer?

Some folks try to stop spam by sending angry replies to spam messages. This approach never works. Often, the "From" line in the spam is left empty, or filled with a dummy or "forged" email address, so a reply won't even reach the real spammer. And when angry replies do reach spammers, they are ignored. It's a program that's sending you this stuff, not a person you can reason with—or intimidate.

Never do anything an unsolicited email tells you to do, even if the instruction claims to be for your benefit.

Many spam messages include "removal" instructions, telling you that if you reply to the message and include the words "REMOVE ME" or a similar phrase in the subject line, you'll receive no further messages. In some cases, doing so may work.

But in many cases, the "REMOVE ME" bit is actually a trick intended to make you to verify your email address. In such cases, following the removal instructions won't remove you from the spammer's list, and may even *increase* the amount of spam you get, because you will have confirmed to the spammer that using your address gets a message through.

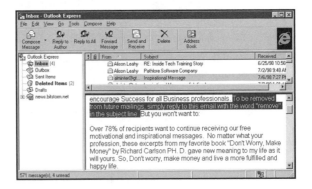

Beyond Survival

Filtering Out Spam

If you can't stop the spam from coming, your next best bet is to avoid having to look at it. A variety of programs and techniques filter your incoming email to remove unwanted messages. Filtering doesn't stop the spammers from sending you messages, but you never have to see them.

You configure filters in your email program to selectively delete or file messages under specified circumstances. For example, if there's a person whose messages you never want to read, you can configure a filter so all messages from that person's email address are deleted automatically upon receipt; you'll never see them.

A filter configured to delete all messages from specified senders is called a kill file.

Note that filters cannot completely remove spam. To set up filters to delete all spam messages, you have to know the address of every spammer. No master list of spammers exists (new folks start spamming every day, and slippery spammers change addresses often).

However, you can pick up lists of many of the worst offenders, and then import or manually copy the lists into your email program so you can create filters to block messages from them.

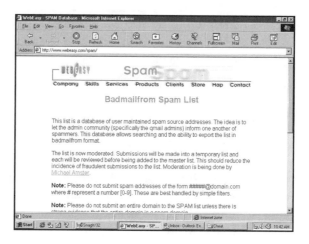

Use the following URLs to learn about and download lists of spammers for filtering:

- The Network Abuse Clearinghouse at `www.abuse.net/`
- Multimedia Marketing Group at `www.mmgco.com/nospam/`
- The Blacklist of Internet Advertisers at `www-math.uni-paderborn.de/%7Eaxel/BL/#list`

About Spam-Killing Programs

Typically, you configure filters in your email program to block unwanted messages, as described next. But you can also purchase utility programs designed to filter out spam.

These utilities combine a filtering system with a spammers database, for fast and easy configuration of anti-spam filters. Check out...

For PC:

- SpamNet at `www.spamnet.com`

- SpamKiller at `novasoft.base.org`

- eFilter at `www.eflash.com`

For Mac:

- SpamBlaster at `www.gooware.com`

Finding Filter Controls in Your Email Program

Most full-featured email programs have their own built-in filtering systems you can apply to manage incoming mail and, to a limited extent, control spam.

If you don't have a list of spammers, or if creating filters for a long list is too difficult, you can deal with spam by creating filters for your legitimate contacts.

It works like this: If you have a steady group of people you communicate with regularly, create a filter that automatically stores all messages from those people in a separate folder. When you receive email, all the important messages are automatically stored in the special folder, while all the spam stays in your Inbox, where you can ignore it.

You can find the filters dialog boxes

- In Messenger, by choosing Edit, Mail Filters.

- In Outlook Express, by choosing Tools, Inbox Assistant.

To configure filters for America Online, choose Mail Controls under the Mail menu.

Even if you use this tip, occasionally scan your Inbox to check for legit messages from new folks not yet added to your filters.

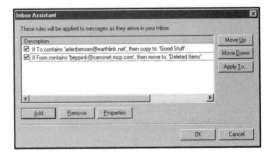

Creating Filters in Messenger

To give you an idea of how to set up filters, the following steps create filters in Messenger that automatically move all messages you receive from your steady email partners into a new folder, leaving any other messages (including spam) behind in your Inbox.

1. From your Messenger Inbox folder, choose File, New Folder to open the New Folder dialog box.

2. Create the folder as a subfolder of Inbox by typing a name (such as "Friends") and clicking OK.

3. Choose Edit, Mail Filters to open the Mail Filters dialog box.

4. Click the New button to open the Filter Rules dialog box.

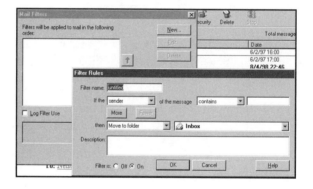

Next you need to create a new filter to move all mail from one of your email partners into the new folder, as described in the next steps.

5. Following "If the," choose sender.

6. Following "of the message," choose contains.

7. In the box to the right of contains, type the email address.

8. Following "then," choose Move to folder.

9. Next to Move to folder, choose the folder you created in step 2.

10. Next to "Filter is" at the bottom of the dialog, choose On.

11. Click OK to save the filter and return to the Mail Filters dialog box.

12. Repeat steps 4–10 for each of your other legitimate email partners.

The Last Resort: Move

When all else fails, if you're still getting too much junk mail, there's one reliable (albeit temporary) solution: Change Internet providers, or ask your current provider to change your email address.

Moving works only if you remember to ask your old ISP not to forward future email to your new address.

When you move or change your email address, spam directed to your old address can't reach you. (Be sure to inform all your legitimate email partners of your new address.) If your address has found its way into lots of spam databases, you can get a clean start this way.

Eventually, spammers will find you. But if you start clean with a new address, and then diligently apply the steps you learned in this chapter, you may be able to keep the spammers at bay.

PART

7

Joining a Discussion

The Internet boasts two different facilities commonly described as "discussion groups" that differ only in the medium on which the discussion takes place.

In the first type of discussion group, *mailing lists*, you read the discussion in email messages you receive and contribute to the discussion by sending email. In the second type of discussion group, *newsgroups*, you read messages on, and send messages to, a *news server*, which automatically distributes the messages to other people in the group.

Regardless of the type you use, discussion groups are a great way to keep up with news about any imaginable topic and to engage in conversation and debate with others online who share your interests.

In this part, you explore discussion group activities, including

- Subscribing to a Mailing List
- Observing Proper Netiquette
- Getting Started with Newsgroups
- Reading and Posting Newsgroup Messages

Cheat Sheet

About the Two Types of Mailing Lists

Most mailing lists are managed not by a person, but by a program called a *Listserv*. Mailing lists managed by people are called *manual* mailing lists, to distinguish them from the lists automated by Listservs. Using each type is a little different from using the other.

Finding a Mailing List

You can use the Web to search for the subscription email address of most mailing lists. Good starting points include

- www.findmail.com
- www.neosoft.com/internet/paml
- www.liszt.com

Subscribing to a Mailing List

Following instructions that appear wherever you locate the subscription address, send a simple email message containing the command required to subscribe to the subscription address.

Usually, you must not only type the correct command, but also type it in a specific place—the message body or Subject line. Read and follow all instructions carefully.

Contributing to a Mailing List

To add your own ideas to the conversation, send a message to the list address. Be careful always to send your contributions to the list address, not the subscription address.

24

Subscribing to a Mailing List

The great thing about mailing lists is that you already know most of what you need to know to use them; you know how to send and receive email. All you need to learn is where and how to find the mailing lists that interest you, how to sign up, and how to quit a mailing list if you lose interest in it.

Basic Survival

About the Two Types of Mailing Lists

For a mailing list to work, someone has to handle its management and administration: mostly signing up new members and removing members who have asked to be removed.

In a few mailing lists, the administration work is handled by a real person. However, most mailing lists are managed not by a person, but by a program called a Listserv.

Sometimes, the mailing lists managed by people are called manual mailing lists, to distinguish them from the lists automated by Listservs.

Finding a Mailing List

The first step in using mailing lists is finding one that interests you. When visiting Web pages devoted to your favorite topics, you'll often see mention of related mailing lists, along with the email addresses required for signing up: the *subscription address*.

Listserv is a generic name for automated lists, but they have several actual names, including Listproc and Majordomo.

You may also visit any of several Web pages that help folks find mailing lists related to a particular subject. A good first stop is FindMail (www.findmail.com), a search tool dedicated to helping you find and use mailing lists.

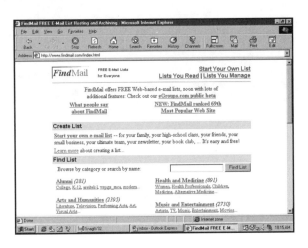

Besides FindMail, other good places to find mailing lists (and instructions for using them) include

- The list of Publicly Accessible Mailing Lists at
  www.neosoft.com/internet/paml

- Liszt, a searchable database of lists and instructions at
  www.liszt.com

- Yahoo!'s directory at
  www.yahoo.com/Computers_and_Internet/Internet/
  Mailing_Lists/

Subscribing to a Mailing List

To use any mailing list, you need to know two different email addresses:

- The address of the person, or Listserv program, that manages the list. This address might be called the "management" or "subscription" address.

- The list address, an email address to which you send all your contributions to the list, the comments or questions you want all others in the list to see.

When you're ready to sign up, you send to the subscription address a simple email message containing the command required to subscribe.

All messages on some mailing lists are automatically copied to a newsgroup on the same topic (see Chapter 26).

Unfortunately, the command for subscribing differs from list to list. Most references to mailing lists—including those you'll turn up in the directories described earlier—include subscription instructions. Those instructions typically tell you the command you must send, and also *where* in the email message—in the Subject line or the message body—you must type that command.

Command instructions use a syntax diagram to tell you what to type. A syntax diagram shows what you must type to properly phrase a command to control a computer program, such as a Listserv.

Even manually managed lists may require a command syntax, but they're more forgiving of mistakes than Listservs.

In a syntax diagram, the exact words you must type are shown in normal type, whereas any parts of the command you must add are surrounded by brackets or shown in italic.

For example, to phrase the command indicated by the syntax diagram

```
subscribe lastname firstname
```

or

```
subscribe [lastname] [firstname]
```

I would type

```
subscribe Snell Ned
```

Notice that you replace anything in italics or enclosed in [ ] or " " with the information indicated, and that you don't really type the [ ] or " ".

To subscribe to a list, read the instructions to find

- The syntax diagram for subscribing
- The part of the message in which to type the command (either the Subject line or body)
- The subscription address

Again, to subscribe, you compose an email message containing only the command indicated by the instructions, and send it to the subscription address.

> **Excerpt from List Info:**
> Working at home amidst being a mom? Telecommuters, Day Care Providers, Professionals, Housewives,
> Full-time at home, Part-time at home, anything that requires Mom's to be working at home, this is your
> list! Come and join our group! To subscribe, send an empty message to wahm-subscribe@makelist.com
> To unsubscribe, send a message to wahm-unsubscribe@makelist.com List Owner: wahm-
> owner@makelist.com [More...]

Reading the Welcome Message

Shortly after you send your subscription message, you'll receive a reply message from the list: a Welcome message.

A Listserv may reply within a minute or two; after sending a subscription message to a Listserv, stay online, wait a few minutes, and then check your email—the reply will probably be there. On the other hand, some Listservs and manual lists may take several days before replying.

A reply may take a day or so. Be patient, and don't resend the subscription just because you don't get a reply right away.

If you did not phrase your subscription message properly, the reply reiterates the subscription command syntax and usually includes instructions. You must compose and send another subscription message, carefully following any instructions in the reply.

After you subscribe successfully, you receive a Welcome message. The Welcome message contains lots of valuable information, particularly

- A syntax diagram for phrasing the command to unsubscribe. If and when you decide you no longer want to receive messages from the list, you'll need to send this command to the subscription address.

Save all Welcome messages, so you can refer to them when you need to know a command or want to unsubscribe.

- The list address to which you must send all your contributions, and the management address (which is usually the same as the subscription address, but not always).

- Syntax for other commands you may use to manage the way messages come to you. For example, many lists let you send a command to temporarily pause—stop sending you messages—if you go on vacation or want messages suspended for any other reason.

- Any other rules or policies all members of the list are required to observe. These typically include the basic rules of netiquette (see Chapter 25, "Observing Proper Netiquette").

Often the Welcome message instructs you to reply to it, to confirm your subscription.

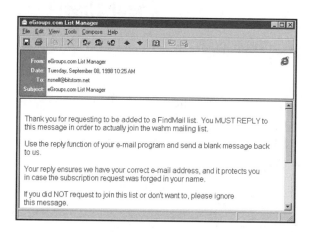

Shortly after you receive the Welcome message (and reply to it, if so instructed), you'll begin receiving email messages from the list. How many and how often depends on the list, but it's not unusual to receive a dozen or more messages per day. Read anything that looks interesting; ignore (or delete) the rest.

Be careful to send your contributions only to the list address, not the subscription address.

Beyond Survival

Contributing to a Mailing List

You are not required to contribute to a mailing list. Many people read and enjoy the messages they receive, and never add their own comments or questions.

If you do feel inspired to contribute, just send a message to the list address. Remember: Always send your contributions to the list address, not the subscription address.

When using Reply to send to a mailing list, double-check the To: line to be sure that it shows the correct list address.

If your contribution is related to a previous message, use your email program's Reply feature to reply to the group, and include in the reply a quote of any portion of the original message that's relevant to your comment or question.

209

Cheat Sheet

Essential Netiquette

Netiquette is a code of conduct, used mainly in message-based discussion groups such as mailing lists and newsgroups, designed to keep the conversation civil and productive. Basic tenets include

- Don't type in ALL CAPITAL LETTERS.
- Stay on topic.
- Keep current on the group's topic.
- Avoid sarcasm.
- Don't post personal messages to the group.
- Don't overuse quotes.
- Write and spell carefully.
- Keep out of arguments (*flames*).

Adding Personality with Smileys and Shorthand

Smileys are little faces made out of letters, numbers, and punctuation. (You have to tilt your head left to see them.) They're used to communicate the tone of a message, to add an emotional inflection.

:-)   :-(:-O

Shorthand abbreviations are used to carry a common phrase efficiently, to save space and typing. Some of these are commonly used offline, everyday, such as ASAP (As Soon As Possible). Another shorthand expression used commonly online is IMO ("In My Opinion") and its cousin, IMHO ("In My Humble Opinion").

25

Observing Proper Netiquette

How you communicate with private friends in email is between you and your friends. But after you begin contributing to discussion groups—mailing lists (refer to Chapter 24, "Subscribing to a Mailing List") and newsgroups (see Chapter 26, "Getting Started with Newsgroups")—you're participating in a public forum, and you have an obligation to follow a code of conduct—*Netiquette*—that keeps the conversation pleasant and productive for all.

Basic Survival

Essential Netiquette

Netiquette can be boiled down to the Golden Rule: Do unto others as you would have others do unto you. As you gain experience, you'll begin to notice things others do that bug you, such as quoting too much or writing sloppily. Obviously, those are the things you must remember not to do yourself.

But to give you a head start, here are the basics of being a good cyber-citizen, particularly in discussion groups. Note that none of this stuff is law; if you skip a rule, the cyber-police will not show up at your door.

Like all forms of courtesy, netiquette is not required, but it's the right thing to do anyway.

- Don't shout. SOME FOLKS LIKE TO TYPE ALL MESSAGES ONLY IN CAPITAL LETTERS, and some others overuse capital letters FOR EMPHASIS! Capitalize normally, and use your word choices and phrasing for emphasis, saving the all-caps trick for rare, EXTREME EMPHASIS.

- Stay on topic. Nothing's more aggravating than subscribing to a list and then receiving all sorts of messages that veer off on tangents. If your message does not pertain directly to the discussion group's stated topic, don't send it.

FAQ =
Frequently
Asked
Questions, a
file containing
answers to
common
questions
pertaining to
a particular
topic or group.

- Keep current. Newcomers to a list or group, or folks who only drop in occasionally, tend to ask questions that have already been asked and answered a dozen times, which annoys the regulars. Keep up with the conversation, so you know what's going on. Read the discussion group's FAQ, if one is made available, so you don't repeat old questions.

- Don't use sarcasm. It's difficult to communicate sarcasm effectively in a written message. Often, exaggerated messages intended as sarcasm are taken literally by those who read them and confusion or arguments ensue. Say what you mean.

- Keep personal discussions personal. Before sending any message, ask yourself: Would this message interest the whole list, or is it really a personal message to just one member? If the message is really for one person, you can find that person's email address in the header information quoted in all list and newsgroup messages, and send your comment or question directly, in private.

- Don't over-quote. When replying, cut quotes down to all that's necessary to show what you're replying to. When a series of replies builds up and nobody cuts the quotes, each message can be pages long even if it contains only one new sentence. Try to leave enough information so a newcomer to the conversation can tell what's being discussed, but cut everything else.

- Write and spell well. In the name of speed and efficiency, some folks boil their msg.s down to a grp. of abbrev.'s &/or shorthnd, or write toooo quikly and slopppilly. Do your readers the courtesy of writing whole words and complete sentences, and fix mistakes before you send.

- Neither flame nor counter-flame. A *flame* is an angry tirade or attack in a message, the kind that flares when a debate grows into a spat. No matter how hot the argument gets, try to keep your cool. When flamed personally, don't rise to the bait: Flame wars only escalate, and no one ever wins.

- Fit in. Usually, I'm no fan of conformity. But every mailing list and newsgroup has its own, insular culture. After reading messages for awhile, you'll pick up a sense of the general technical level of the group, whether they're experts or novices (or both) on the topic at hand, the overall tone, catchphrases, vocabulary, and so on.

- By all means, be yourself. Any group needs fresh ideas, new personalities. But try to be yourself within the style and culture of the group to ensure that you can be understood by all.

Beyond Survival

Adding Personality with Smileys and Shorthand

Over the years, a system of symbols and shorthand has developed to enable folks to be more expressive in their messages: smileys and shorthand. You'll see both used online, in discussion groups, in email, and when chatting.

Smileys are used to communicate the tone of a message, to add an emotional inflection. They're little pictures, usually of faces, that are built out of text characters.

To see the picture, you tilt your head to the left. For example, tilt your head to the left (or tilt this book to the right) while looking at the smiley below, which is made up of three characters: a colon, a dash and a close parenthesis:

    :-)

Looks like a little smiling face, doesn't it? Folks follow a statement with this smiley to indicate that the statement is a joke or that it is facetious—for example:

```
Just for that, I'm leaving you everything in my
will. :-)
```

There are many different smileys, some so obscure that only the real net jocks use or understand them. But you're likely only to see the basics, including the basic smile shown earlier and also:

:-(	Frowning
;-)	Winking
:-0	Surprised
8-)	Smiling with glasses or Bug–eyed
:'-(	Crying
:-D	Laughing

Some folks omit the nose from their smileys; for example:
:) ;) :0

Shorthand abbreviations are used to carry a common phrase efficiently, to save space and typing. Some of these are commonly used offline, everyday, such as ASAP ("As Soon As Possible"). Another shorthand expression used commonly online is IMO ("In My Opinion") and its cousin, IMHO ("In My Humble Opinion"). For example:

```
The Godfather is the greatest film of the '70s,
IMHO.
```

Watch out for over-using shorthand, which can make your message look like code.

Other popular shorthand expressions include:

- BTW: By The Way
- B4: Before
- FWIW: For What It's Worth
- IBTD: I Beg To Differ
- IOW: In Other Words
- LOL: Laughing Out Loud (generally used to declare that a statement is laughable)
- OTOH: On The Other Hand
- ROTFL: Rolling On The Floor Laughing (generally used to declare that a statement is extremely laughable)
- TTFN: Tah-Tah For Now (goodbye, I'm signing off)

214

Cheat Sheet

About Newsgroups and Newsreaders

A newsreader program retrieves messages from and posts messages to
Internet newsgroups, sometimes known as discussion groups or Usenet.
The newsgroups and their messages are stored on a family of servers called
news servers or NNTP servers.

Your ISP or online service has a news server you are authorized to use for
reading and contributing to newsgroups.

Configuring Your Newsreader

Before you can open newsgroups and display their messages, you must
configure your newsreader to contact your ISP's news server. Newsreaders
have a configuration dialog box on which you enter the information
required for communicating with your ISP's news server:

- In Collabra, choose Edit, Preferences to open the Preferences dialog
  box. In the list of Categories, choose Mail & Groups.
- In Outlook Express, complete the News dialog boxes of the
  Connection Wizard (see Chapter 6, "Connecting to the Internet").

Downloading the Newsgroups List

After your newsreader knows how to contact the server, you must download the complete list of newsgroups. If you open some newsreaders
(including Collabra and Outlook Express) without first having downloaded the list, a prompt appears, asking whether you want to download
the list.

Finding and Subscribing to Newsgroups

After the list has been downloaded to your computer, you can find and
subscribe to any newsgroups you want. Newsgroups are organized under a
system of names and categories.

Organizing Messages

Newsreaders let you arrange the messages in the list in various ways. Often
the most useful way is by thread. A thread is a single conversation: a message, all replies to that message, and all replies to the replies.

26

Getting Started with Newsgroups

Newsgroups carry pretty much the same discussions that mailing lists do. In fact, many mailing lists and newsgroups covering the same topic carry the very same conversation; they're hooked together so all messages sent to either the mailing list or the newsgroup show up in both.

But unlike mailing lists, newsgroups don't come to you—you go to them. Here's how.

Basic Survival

About Newsgroups & Newsreaders

When you know how to use an email program, you know 90% of what you need to know to use newsgroups. Reading a message, composing a new message, and replying are all similar in an email program and a newsreader.

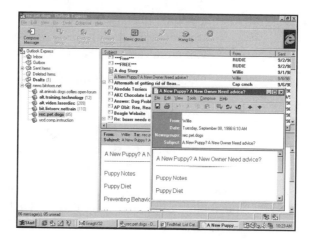

Where a newsreader differs, of course, is that it retrieves messages from, and posts messages to, Internet newsgroups, sometimes known as discussion groups or *Usenet*. The newsgroups and their messages are stored on a family of servers called news servers or NNTP servers.

Sending a message to a newsgroup is known as posting.

Your ISP or online service has a news server you are authorized to use for reading and contributing to newsgroups. Access to one news server is all you need; the messages sent to any news server on the Internet are automatically copied—at regular intervals—to all news servers.

On any news server, you can open any newsgroup and read any current message posted to that newsgroup, no matter which news server the message was originally posted to. That's why a newsgroup on an ISP's server in New York has messages on it from folks in Canada, California, and the United Kingdom.

Configuring Your Newsreader

Before you can open newsgroups and display their messages, you must configure your newsreader to contact your ISP's news server, and you must download the complete list of newsgroups from the server.

As with other types of clients, there are many different newsreaders out there. In the Big Internet suites, the programs are called

If you use America Online, you may be required to use the online service inter- face for newsgroups.

- Collabra, in Netscape Communicator. You can open Collabra from within the Navigator browser by choosing Communicator, Collabra Discussion Groups.

- Outlook Express, in Internet Explorer 4. Yep, it's the same program you use for email. You click your news server's name near the bottom of the folder list to shift Outlook Express into newsgroup mode. You can open Outlook Express directly in newsgroup mode by choosing Go, News from within the browser.

If you don't already have a newsreader, you may apply the file-finding techniques from Part 5, "Finding Other Stuff," to search for one, or browse a directory of newsreaders on Yahoo! at

```
www.yahoo.com/Computers_and_Internet/Software/
Internet/Usenet/
```

In Outlook Express, choosing the news server changes toolbar buttons and menu choices to ones for newsgroups.

All newsreaders have a configuration dialog box on which you enter the information required for communicating with your ISP's news server. That dialog box always requires the address of your ISP's news server. If your newsreader is not part of a suite (and thus cannot copy configuration information from the email component), the configuration dialog box also requires your email address and full name.

You'll find the configuration dialog box:

- For Collabra, by choosing Edit, Preferences to open the Preferences dialog box. In the list of Categories, choose Mail & Groups. Complete the configuration settings in the Mail & Groups category's Groups Server subcategory.

- For Outlook Express, by completing the News dialog boxes of the Connection Wizard (see Chapter 6). If you choose your news server folder in Outlook Express without having configured first, the Connection Wizard opens automatically.

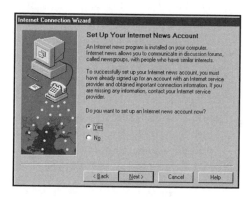

Downloading the Newsgroups List

After your newsreader knows how to contact the server, you must download the complete list of newsgroups, which usually takes just a few minutes. If you open some newsreaders (including Collabra and Outlook Express) without first having downloaded the list, a prompt appears, asking whether you want to download the list.

219

If your newsreader does not prompt you, find a button or menu item for downloading the list:

- In Collabra, click the Subscribe button on the toolbar. On the dialog box that appears, click the Get Groups button.

- In Outlook Express, click the name of your news server, and then choose Tools, Newsgroups. On the dialog box that appears, click Reset List.

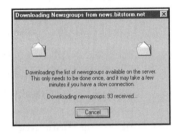

If your news-reader does not detect list changes, download the list once a month, to keep current.

The list of newsgroups changes frequently, adding new groups and removing others. Collabra, Outlook Express, and some other newsreaders detect automatically when the list changes and display a prompt, asking whether you want to update your list.

Finding and Subscribing to Newsgroups

After the list has been downloaded to your computer, you can find and subscribe to any newsgroups you want. While exploring Web pages devoted to topics that interest you, you'll probably come across the names of related newsgroups. But newsgroups are easy to find, with or without a Web page's help.

Newsgroups are organized under a system of names and categories. The leftmost portion of the name shows the top-level category in which the group resides; each portion further to the right more narrowly determines the subject of the group.

For example, the top-level category rec contains *rec*reational newsgroups, those dedicated to a recreational—rather than professional—discussion of their topics. So the hypothetical newsgroup name

```
rec.sports.basketball.womens
```

indicates that the discussion focuses on a recreational interest in women's basketball. There are thousands of rec groups, many rec.sports groups, several rec.sports.basketball groups, but just one rec.sports.basketball.womens newsgroup.

Some of the other major top-level categories are

- alt. Alternative newsgroups, those in which the most free-wheeling conversations are accepted.

- biz. Business newsgroups and ads.

- comp. Computer-related newsgroups.

- k12. Education-related groups.

- misc. Miscellaneous.

- sci. Science-related groups.

Alt groups permit the most sexual content and other "adult" stuff, but also have plenty of "wholesome" content.

Using Collabra to Open a Newsgroup

To subscribe to and open groups in Collabra:

1. Open Collabra, and display the newsgroup list. It appears automatically right after you download the full list, but you can redisplay it at any time by clicking the Subscribe button.

2. In the All Groups tab, display the group's name in the Discussion Group box. There are several ways to do this:

   - If you know the exact name of the group you want to subscribe to, type the name in the box.

   - Use the list to scroll to the group name, then click it. In the list, the groups are presented alphabetically and also organized by category; display a category's subcategories or groups by clicking the plus sign (+) that precedes it.

   - Click the Search for a Group tab, and enter a search term to locate group names containing the term. Click the name of the group you want to subscribe to.

If you don't
see news-
groups listed
under your
server, click
the plus sign
(+) to the
left of the
server name.

3. When the name of the group you want to subscribe to appears in the Discussion Group box, click the Subscribe button to subscribe to it. You can then select another group to subscribe to, or click OK to close the dialog box.

4. In the Message Center (which appears whenever you open Collabra), your subscribed newsgroups are listed. To open a newsgroup, double-click its name in the list.

Using Outlook Express to Open a Newsgroup

To subscribe to and open groups in Outlook Express:

1. Display the newsgroup list. It appears automatically right after you download the full list, but you can redisplay it at any time by choosing Tools, Newsgroups.

2. The list dialog box has three tabs: All, Subscribed, and New. Choose the All tab, to display the full list.

3. To find a newsgroup, you can scroll down the alphabetical list. To locate a group about a particular topic, type a word related to that topic in the box at the top of the dialog box; Outlook Express narrows the list to groups whose names include that word.

4. When you see the name of a group you want to subscribe to in the list, click the group name to select it.

5. Click the Subscribe button to subscribe to the selected newsgroup. You can now select and subscribe to another group, or click OK to close the dialog box.

6. The name of your news server appears near the bottom of Outlook Express's folder list, along the left side of the window. Click it, and your subscribed newsgroups appear in the main pane. To open a newsgroup and display its current message list, click it.

Beyond Survival

Organizing Messages

Most newsreaders let you arrange the messages in the list in myriad ways—alphabetically by subject, by author, by date, and so on. (The options for sorting the message list in Collabra,

Outlook Express, and most other Windows and Mac newsreaders appear on the View menu.) The most useful sorting, however, is by thread.

A thread is one conversation— a message, all replies to that message, replies to the replies, and so on.

In effect, threads group messages by subject. But two messages can have the same subject but not the same thread, if neither is a reply to the other (or a reply to a reply to the other). If you sort messages by thread, and then by subject, you'll get all threads on a given subject grouped together.

When you sort messages by thread, you can follow the flow of the conversation, and click your way, in order, through the messages to see how the discussion has progressed.

In many newsreaders, when messages are sorted by threads, the replies to a message do not appear automatically in the list; instead, a plus sign (+) appears next to the message's listing, to indicate that there are submessages—replies—to that message. To display the replies, click the plus sign.

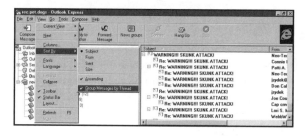

Cheat Sheet

Reading Newsgroup Messages

Reading messages through a newsreader is just like reading email messages in an email client. In Collabra or Outlook Express, single-click an item in the list to display it in the preview pane, or double-click it to display the message in its own window.

Composing Messages

You compose and reply to messages in a newsreader exactly as you do in an email program (refer to Chapter 21, "Composing and Sending Email"), only the terminology is different:

- In email, you click Send to send a message; in a newsreader, it's either Send or Post.
- In email, you click Reply to reply to a message; in a newsreader, it's either Reply or Respond.

Posting Replies

When replying, open the message to which you want to reply; then click the Reply (or Respond) button in the message window in which that message appears.

Replying in Private

Most newsreaders provide the option of replying to the newsgroup or sending an email reply directly to the author of the message you're replying to, when your message is intended only for the original message's author, not the whole group.

Finding and Reading Newsgroup Messages Through Your Browser

Many Web browsers display newsgroup messages, but most don't let you post, so you still need a newsreader to really get into newsgroups. A Web browser's display capability comes in handy when a search tool turns up a link that leads to a newsgroup message.

27

Reading and Posting Newsgroup Messages

After you've completed all the setup steps in Chapter 26, "Getting Started with Newsgroups," you're ready to explore newsgroups—and there's plenty to explore, more than you'll ever have time for. Here's how to do it.

Basic Survival

Reading Newsgroup Messages

Reading messages through a newsreader is just like reading email messages in an email client.

In Collabra or Outlook Express, single-click an item in the list to display it in the preview pane, or double-click it to display the message in its own window.

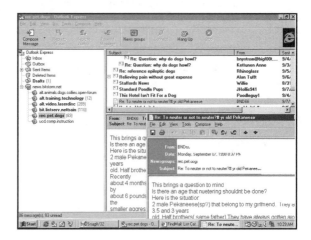

Why Do Messages Take So Long to Appear?

The message lists you see in an email program generally show messages that have been copied to your computer. But the messages in the list you see when you open a newsgroup are not on your computer; they're on the news server.

The only items that have been copied to your computer are the message headers, to make up the list. When you display any particular message, that message is then copied to your computer. Because the messages aren't copied until you request them, you must stay online while working with newsgroups.

Downloading all messages in a busy newsgroup can take a long time.

Some newsreaders support *offline news reading*; you can configure them to automatically download messages from newsgroups so you can read them later, offline. In Outlook Express, you can download all messages from a newsgroup by choosing Tools, Download All.

Composing Messages

You compose and reply to messages in a newsreader exactly as you do in an email program. The only real difference is in the To line of the message header, because instead of addressing a message to a person, you're addressing it to a newsgroup.

The only other difference is the terminology you see applied on buttons and menu items:

- In email, you click Send to send a message; in a newsreader, it's either Send or Post.

- In email, you click Reply to reply to a message; in a newsreader, it's either Reply or Respond.

When composing messages to a newsgroup, mind your netiquette (refer to Chapter 25).

The easiest way to deal with that difference is to start in the right place.

For example, when you want to compose a new message (not a reply) and post it on a newsgroup, open the newsgroup, and then click your newsreader's button for composing a new message (it's New Msg in Collabra, Compose Message in Outlook Express). When the message window opens, you'll see that it's preaddressed to the currently open newsgroup.

Posting Replies

When replying, open the message to which you want to reply; then click the Reply (or Respond) button on the message window in which that message appears.

In the message window that opens, the message is preaddressed to the appropriate newsgroup, the subject line is correctly phrased to add the reply to the same thread as the original message, and the original message is quoted in the message area. Just add your comments, and edit the quote as necessary.

After completing a new message or reply, send the message by clicking the button or menu item labeled Send or Post.

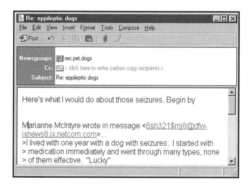

Beyond Survival

Replying in Private

When you choose to reply, most newsreaders provide the option of replying to the newsgroup or sending an email reply directly to the author of the message you're replying to. For example, Outlook Express's toolbar offers two reply buttons while you're viewing a newsgroup message:

- The Reply to Group button sends a reply to be posted on the newsgroup.

- The Reply to Author button sends a reply via email to only the author of the message you're reading, not to the group.

The email option is handy when your reply is really intended only as a private response to the author of the message, not for public display on the newsgroup.

Finding and Reading Newsgroup Messages Through Your Browser

Many Web browsers can display newsgroup messages. You can't use a Web browser to contribute to a newsgroup, however, so you'll still need a newsreader to really get into newsgroups.

A Web browser's display capability comes in handy when a search tool turns up a newsgroup message. Newsgroup messages show up in a search tool's hot list as links; if your browser can display newsgroup messages, clicking one of those links displays the message.

Try using a search tool to find and display a newsgroup message in your browser:

In some browsers, clicking a link to a newsgroup message opens the companion newsreader.

1. Open your Web browser, and go to Alta Vista at `altavista.digital.com`.

2. Click the Search drop-down list above the search term box.

3. From the list, choose Usenet to instruct Alta Vista to find newsgroup messages instead of Web pages.

4. In the search term box, type a term for a topic you're interested in.

5. Click Search. The hit list appears, showing links to newsgroup messages. The link is also the subject of the message; the name of the group on which the message was posted appears to the right of the link.

6. Click a link. The message appears in your browser, or in your newsreader if your browser opens it automatically.

PART

8

Live Communication

Through the Internet, you can communicate "live" with others in several different ways.

Netscape Communicator and Internet Explorer 4 both include a program for live, real-time conferencing through the Net. In Communicator it's called Conference, and in Internet Explorer it's called NetMeeting, but no matter: The two programs are very similar. With one of these programs, you can have a live conversation—very much like a telephone call—with anyone else on the Internet who uses the same conferencing program that you do.

Another way to communicate live is to join a *chat* session, a live conversation in which two or more participants interact through typed messages.

In this part, you explore live communications activities, including

- Getting Started with Voice and Video Conferencing
- Using NetMeeting
- Understanding Internet Relay Chat
- Joining a Chat
- Contributing to a Chat

Cheat Sheet

How It Works—and Doesn't Work

As a rule, those with whom you share a conference must use the same conferencing program you do. Using NetMeeting, you can conference only with other NetMeeting users. Ditto Netscape's Conference.

Where Do You Get the Software?

Microsoft NetMeeting and Netscape Conference are included in their respective suites. You can also download them and other Internet conferencing programs.

Hardware You Need

To have a voice conference, you must have the following equipment installed and configured in your computer:

- A sound card
- A microphone, either attached to your sound card or built-in to your computer
- Speakers or headphones

Setting Up for Conferencing

Before you can use a conferencing program, you must supply it with a little information to configure communications. The first time you start Conference or NetMeeting, the program launches a Setup Wizard to collect this information from you.

Getting Started with Voice and Video Conferencing

Conferencing is a very different animal from the Internet activities you've explored thus far. Before venturing into conferencing, it's useful to understand a little more about how it works.

Basic Survival

How It Works—and Doesn't Work

Most Internet activities are *standardized*; that is, they're based on agreed-upon rules than enable all different programs and systems to interact. For example, because of standards, you can send a message with one email program, and your recipient can read it in another; the difference in programs doesn't matter, because all Internet email programs follow the same standards.

Conferencing has yet to be standardized (although standardization efforts are underway). For that reason—although there are a few, minor exceptions—those with whom you share a conference must use the same conferencing program you do. Using NetMeeting, you can conference only with other NetMeeting users. The same is true for Netscape's Conference.

Netscape's Conference supports the H.323 standard that enables different programs to talk together when both support H.323.

Obviously, this is a severe limitation; you typically cannot dial up any friend on the Internet and conference. Rather, you must first contact your conferencing partners by phone or email and agree upon what conferencing software you will use when you call one another.

Where Do You Get the Software?

Microsoft NetMeeting and Netscape Conference are included in their respective suites. You can also download them.

Get NetMeeting at

```
www.microsoft.com/netmeeting/
```

To include NetMeeting automatically when installing IE4, choose "Full" when prompted to select an "Installation Option."

Get Conference at:

```
home.netscape.com/comprod/products/communicator/
conference.html
```

Other popular conferencing programs include:

- Internet Phone: www.vocaltec.com

- PowWow: www.tribal.com/powwow

You can find other conferencing programs in Yahoo!'s Internet Telephone programs directory at:

```
www.yahoo.com/Business_and_Economy/Companies/
Computers/Software/Internet/Internet_Phone/Titles/
```

Hardware You Need

The most popular form of conferencing through these products is voice conferencing—speaking and listening just as you would in a telephone call. You can also have a video conference (see Chapter 29, "Using NetMeeting").

To have a voice conference, you must have the following equipment installed and configured in your computer:

- A sound card

- A microphone, either attached to your sound card or built in to your computer. In a voice conference, you speak into the mike.

- Speakers or headphones, attached to your sound card or built in to your computer. You'll hear your partner's words through the speakers or headphones.

The sound quality of voice conferences is highly variable; an Internet voice conference never sounds as clear as a phone call, even on the best equipment. Still, it's important to know that the better your equipment, the clearer the call will sound.

External mikes are better than built-in ones, which often pick up too much background noise from the computer.

In particular, more expensive, 32-bit sound cards enable a much clearer conversation than cheaper, 16-bit or 8-bit cards (although those will work).

The speed of your Internet connection also plays a role. The faster your connection, the clearer the conversation.

Connections of 28.8k or faster provide acceptable sound; on slower connections, you'll hear heavy static and occasional interruptions. For the best sound quality through the Net, use a 56k connection.

Beyond Survival

Setting Up for Conferencing

Before you can use a conferencing program, you must supply it with a little information. The first time you start Conference or NetMeeting, for example, the program launches a Setup Wizard to collect this information from you. Just work your way through the steps to configure your conferencing program.

To illustrate a typical setup procedure, here are the steps for setting up Microsoft's NetMeeting. (Note that setting up Netscape's Conference is nearly identical.)

1. Open NetMeeting by choosing Programs, Internet Explorer, Microsoft NetMeeting from the Windows Start menu. The wizard opens.

2. Read the introductory message, and then click on the Next button to get started.

   The first thing you need to decide is whether you want to log on to a NetMeeting directory server when you start the application, and if so, which one. In most cases, this is a good idea because the directory server is where you will probably find the people you want to talk to.

   I suggest leaving the Log on to a directory server when NetMeeting starts check box checked and leaving the What directory server you would like to use? list set to uls.microsoft.com for now. You can change both options later if you need to.

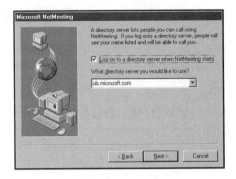

When filling in an identification dialog box in a communications program, don't type anything you want to keep private.

3. Choose your server options, and then click Next.

NetMeeting wants to know some things about you. This information will show up on the directory server that you chose in the preceding dialog box whenever you are logged on.

4. Type the information that you want to have listed, and click the Next button to continue.

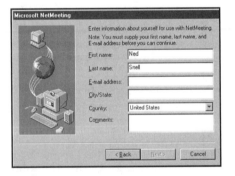

5. On the next dialog box, you decide which category in the directory to list yourself in: personal use, business use, or adults-only use. Choose the option that is appropriate for how you intend to use NetMeeting, and then click the Next button to continue. A dialog box informing you that you're about to configure your sound card for NetMeeting opens.

6. Click Next. A dialog box opens, listing your sound card as the *wave device* (sound card) that NetMeeting will use for recording (sending your voice to others) and playback (playing others' voices to you).

7. If the device listed is your sound card, click Next. Otherwise, use the drop-down lists to select the correct devices, and then click Next.

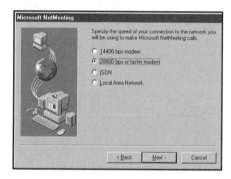

8. Next you tell NetMeeting what type of connection to the Internet you have. Click the correct option, and then click Next. A dialog box appears in which you help NetMeeting set the microphone level so the people you talk to can hear you clearly.

9. Click the Start Recording button, and then immediately begin reading the paragraph that begins "Microsoft NetMeeting enables you to...", speaking clearly and as loudly as you would speak during a voice call in NetMeeting. NetMeeting records your voice for about nine seconds, using its strength to set a recording level for future NetMeeting sessions.

10. When the Tuning Progress indicator reaches the end, NetMeeting stops recording. Don't worry if you haven't finished reading the paragraph; just click the Next button to continue.

11. A final dialog box appears, reporting that you've config-ured NetMeeting. Click Finish to close the wizard.

NetMeeting starts and logs on to the directory server you chose. After you're logged on, you see a list of other users who are logged on to the same server. You can scroll through the list (which is sorted by email address) and find your name in there. Now anyone who wants to talk to you can find your name on the list and call you.

Cheat Sheet

Understanding the Directory Listing

When you first start NetMeeting, you see a list of people who are in the Category and server you selected when you ran the NetMeeting Setup Wizard.

The Window Buttons

To the left of the directory listing are four buttons: Directory, SpeedDial, Current Call, and History.

Answering a Call

When someone calls you, if you're online and have NetMeeting open, you hear a "ringing" coming out of the speakers of your computer. At the bottom right side of your screen, a dialog box says who is calling.

Placing a Call

To set up and start a call, prearrange the conference via email or by other means. In NetMeeting, log on to your partner's directory server. Find your partner's name in the listing, and then double-click the name to make the call.

Videoconferencing

After a computer video camera has been installed and configured in a Windows or Mac operating system, NetMeeting automatically senses and uses it. If your partner has a camera, the image from that camera appears in a small square on the right side of the Current Call dialog box. If you have a camera installed, your NetMeeting partner sees you.

Text Chatting

Text chatting is using your conferencing software to conduct a conversation through a series of typed messages, instead of by voice or video.

Whiteboard

Click the Whiteboard button while in a call, and a separate window opens—the *whiteboard*—a space in which you can draw and jot notes.

29

Using NetMeeting

After your conferencing software is all set up (as described in Chapter 28, "Getting Started with Voice and Video Conferencing"), you can begin to conference with friends and associates, near and far. Here's how to start in Microsoft's NetMeeting; note that using Netscape's Conference is very similar.

Understanding the Directory Listing

When you first start NetMeeting, you see a list of people. These are the people in the Category you selected and on the server you selected when you ran the NetMeeting Setup Wizard (see Chapter 28).

Because I chose ils.microsoft.com as my server and put myself in the For Personal Use category, I can see the list of everyone who made the same choices.

In this list, you see eight columns:

- E-mail. The person's email address.
- Audio. A small yellow speaker in this column means that this person can talk to you.

- Video. A small gray video camera in this column means that this person can send live video over the Internet.

- First Name. The person's first name.

- Last Name. The person's last name.

- City/State. The city and state in which this person is currently located.

- Country. The country in which this person is located.

- Comments. Comments, if any, that this person entered in the comments field.

Using Category and Server Lists

Above the directory listing are the Category and Server drop-down lists. These control who shows up in the directory listing. When you start NetMeeting, by default it logs you on to the server you chose in the NetMeeting Setup Wizard and displays the category you chose for your entry.

If you want to see the entries on a different server, just click the down-arrow to the right of the Server drop-down list and choose the server that you want to use.

Similarly, to see the list of people in a different category than yourself, just choose the category you want to see from the Category drop-down list. Setting the Category field to, say, Business, lets you see the list of people who have designated that their information is For Business Use.

The Window Buttons

To the left of the directory listing are four buttons, each of which opens a new dialog box:

- Directory

- SpeedDial

- Current Call

- History

The Directory contains the Category and Server fields and the directory listing. The first time you start NetMeeting, the Directory is what you see. Clicking the other button enables you to see different information pertaining to calls you can make, the current call, or calls you've received.

Using the audio level controls, you can change the level of your voice and the voice of the other person on the call.

You can use the options on the SpeedDial dialog box the same way you use a SpeedDial button on your telephone. This dialog box keeps a short list of people you call regularly so you don't have to search for their names in the main directory listing. You can also have people who frequent different servers on the same SpeedDial list so you don't have to keep changing servers to find the person you want to call.

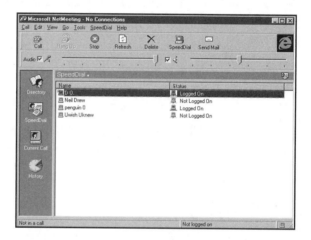

The Current Call dialog box shows a list of the people in the current call. You will always find at least two names in this list if you're in a call, or none if you're not. Also, if you or another person is sending video, you'll see it in the video boxes on the right side of the screen on this dialog box.

Finally, the History dialog box holds a list of all the calls you've received from other people. The caller's name, the date and time of the call, and whether you accepted, rejected, or ignored the call are all listed on this dialog box.

Answering a Call

To talk to someone on the Internet with NetMeeting, you have to call someone or someone has to call you. In this section you learn how to answer a call; in the next section you learn how to make a call.

When someone calls you, the first thing that happens is you hear the phone ring. It's not really the phone ringing, however; the sound is coming out of the speakers of your computer. Next, you'll notice at the bottom right side of your screen a NetMeeting dialog box that says who is calling. It has two buttons: Accept and Ignore.

To ignore someone calling you, click the Ignore button. To answer a call, click the Accept button.

After you accept a call, the NetMeeting window switches automatically to the Current Call dialog box. Here you'll see the name of the caller and your name, along with a little information. To the right of each name are several columns:

- **Audio.** A little yellow speaker in this column means that this person can talk over the Internet.

- **Video.** A small gray video camera in this column means that you should also see live video in the Remote Video frame to the right.

- **Chat.** A small white and blue rectangle in this column means that the chat window is open.

To learn more about NetMeeting's Chat and Video features, see the "Beyond Survival" section in this chapter.

It may take a few seconds for NetMeeting to complete the connection between your computer and the caller's. After it has finished, however, start gabbing—your conference is underway.

When you finish talking to the caller, one of you has to hang up. In NetMeeting, this means clicking the Hang Up button on the toolbar. You can hang up at any time, just like you can on the telephone.

Placing a Call

Calling someone with NetMeeting is actually easier than using the white pages and a telephone. You don't need to remember or dial anyone's phone number, you just have to double-click a name in the directory list. After you've connected with someone, you can have NetMeeting automatically save the listing for you.

1. Prearrange the conference, via email or other means.

2. In NetMeeting, log on to the directory server where your partner is listed.

3. Find your partner's name in the listing.

4. Double-click the name to make the call.

Beyond Survival

**Videocon-
ferencing**

Few conferencing programs today support videoconferencing, and for good reason: It doesn't work very well.

Making live video look good requires moving and processing tons of data very quickly, and even the fastest modems and computers are not quite up to the task. The video image you'll see of your conference partner (and the one they'll see of you) is small, fuzzy and jerky, like watching a bad station on a two-inch TV in a thunderstorm.

Besides not always looking so good, video-conferencing often degrades the audio quality in the call.

That said, setting up and using video in NetMeeting—one of the few programs that supports it—is a breeze. All you really need to do is install a computer video camera on your PC or Mac. These cameras—usually designed to sit on your desk or mount on top of your monitor—come in color and black-and-white models, and can cost less than $100.

After a video camera has been installed and configured in your Windows or Mac OS, NetMeeting automatically senses and takes advantage of it. If your partner has a video camera installed, the image from that camera automatically appears in a small square on the right side of the Current Call dialog box; the Remote Video Frame. If you have a camera installed, your partner also sees you.

**Text
Chatting**

Text chatting is using your conferencing software to conduct a conversation through a series of typed messages, just like using Chat (see Chapter 30, "Understanding Internet Relay Chat").

Why would anybody have a text chat instead of a voice chat? Well, several reasons come to mind:

A text con-ference is similar to, but not the same as, IRC Chat (see Chapter 30).

- One or more of the participants is speech- or hearing-impaired.

- One or more of the participants has insufficient hardware, or too slow a connection, to support a voice conference. Text conferences require no sound card and work fine over slow connections.

243

- The conference requires the input of more than two participants. Voice- and videoconferences are limited to parties of two, although a text chat can include three, four, or more participants.

To hold a text chat in Conference or NetMeeting, you establish the call just as you would for a voice conference. All participants then switch to text chat mode by clicking the Chat button. Everyone types whatever they have to say, and all statements typed by all participants appear in a scrolling display in the conference program. Each statement is labeled with the name of the speaker, so everybody knows who said what.

Whiteboard Ever been in a meeting where someone feels he needs to present his idea visually, so he jumps up and starts drawing on a blackboard, or the more modern office "whiteboard"?

In NetMeeting and Conference, you can do the same thing. Click the Whiteboard button while in a call, and a separate window opens—the whiteboard—a space in which you can draw and jot notes. Whatever anyone in the call draws on the whiteboard appears to all participants, so partners can even add to one another's drawings.

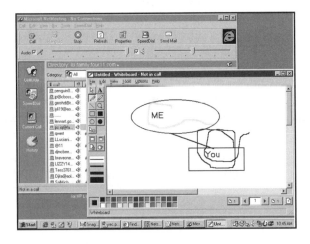

Cheat Sheet

Understanding Internet Chatting

A chat takes place on a chat server, more properly called an *IRC server*. Just as you need a Web browser to communicate with a Web server, you need a chat client, such as Microsoft Chat, to communicate with a chat server.

When you're in a chat room, everything you type in your chat client appears on the screen of everybody else participating in that particular chat, and vice versa.

About Microsoft Chat

Internet Explorer 4's own chat client, included in the full installation (refer to Chapter 3, "What Software Do You Need?"), is called Microsoft Chat. Chat makes the chat session look like a comic strip, just for fun.

Web Chatting

Web chatting is another kind of chat. A Web chat takes place within a Web page, and is generally hosted as a discussion related to the Web page's topic. To join a Web chat with your browser, you need the right plug-in for the type of Web chat underway.

30

Understanding Internet Relay Chat

Internet Relay Chat (IRC)—nicknamed just chat—puts you online in a live conversation with other Internet users, anywhere in the world. To use chat, you need a program called a chat client.

Many chat clients are available. The one Microsoft offers for free, Microsoft Chat, does everything most chat clients do— plus one more, fun feature. For that reason, you'll discover Internet chatting in this chapter (and in the following two chapters, too) principally through Microsoft Chat. (Netscape Communicator does not include a chat client, but you can download and use Microsoft Chat—or any other chat client— right alongside Communicator.)

Basic Survival

Understanding Internet Chatting

A chat takes place on a chat server, more properly called an IRC server. (IRC stands for Internet Relay Chat, the full formal name for Chat.) Just as you need a Web browser to communicate with a Web server, you need a chat client to communicate with a chat server.

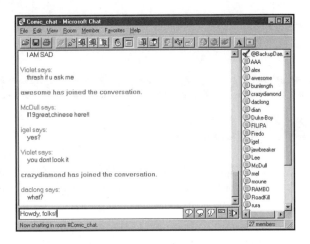

When you're in an Internet chat, everything you type in your chat client appears on the screen of everybody else participating in that particular chat. Thousands of different chats are underway at once, each in its own chat room. When you join a chat, you enter a room, and from then on you see only the conversation that's taking place in that room.

In most chat rooms, the conversation is focused around a given subject area. In a singles chat room, participants chat about stuff singles like to talk about. In a geology chat, people generally talk about rocks and earthquakes.

> Your self-chosen nickname is how you're known to others in a chat; it appears on every statement you make.

When you're in a chat room, everything anyone else in the same room types appears on your screen. Each participant's statements are labeled with a nickname to identify who's talking. Those participating in a chat (known as *members*) choose their own nicknames and rarely share their real names. In a chat, you can be whoever you want to be, and so can everyone else.

Why Is Chat "The Most Dangerous Place on the Net"?

You may as well know right now that a substantial amount of chat traffic on the Internet is dedicated to sex chats of various persuasions and fetishes. Many sex chat rooms exist, and sex-chat-oriented chatters often wander into non-sex-oriented rooms looking for new, um, "friends."

More about kids, chat, and safety in Part 9, "Making the Most of the Internet."

If you have an aversion to such stuff, tread carefully in Chat. If you have a severe aversion to it, it's best to stay out of Chat altogether. You can find a lot of other stuff to do on the Net.

Regardless of your own interests, I strongly advise against permitting children to use Chat, especially unsupervised. My warning isn't about sex—it's about safety.

Beyond Survival

About Microsoft Chat

Internet Explorer 4's own chat client, included in the full installation (refer to Chapter 3), is called Microsoft Chat, and it's an unusual animal.

If you don't have Microsoft Chat, but want it, download it from

```
www.microsoft.com/ie/chat
```

To learn about or download other chat clients, apply the file searching techniques from Part 5, "Finding Other Stuff," or check out the Tucows Internet software library at

```
tucows.mcp.com
```

Like any chat client, Microsoft Chat—from now on referred to as *Chat* with a capital *C*—lets you communicate with chat servers. You can view the list of chat rooms, join a chat room, read what everyone says in the chat room, and make your own contributions to the discussion.

Others in the chat room see your statements as regular text—not comics—if they're not using Microsoft Chat.

What's different about Chat is the way it displays the conversation. Like the chat client shown earlier (which is really just Chat in its text mode), most chat clients show the text of the conversation, a line at a time, and label each line with the speaker's nickname.

Chat, however, displays the conversation like a comic strip, using little cartoon characters to represent members and showing the members' words in cartoon word balloons.

On your display, Chat converts all statements in a chat—even those made by users of text-only clients—into comics. Other Chat users in the room with you appear as their chosen cartoon characters. For users of other chat clients, Chat automatically assigns and shows an unused character.

Web Chatting

A Web chat takes place within a Web page, and is generally hosted as a discussion related to the Web page's topic.

To join a Web chat with your browser, you need the right plug-in for the type of Web chat that is underway. Several types of plug-ins are available, but most Web chats are supported by the ichat plug-in. You'll usually find a link for downloading ichat on the Web page where a chat takes place. But you can also get ichat from the source:

www.ichat.com

Cheat Sheet

Opening Chat and Connecting to a Server

1. Open Microsoft Chat. (In Windows 95/98, choose Programs, Internet Explorer, Microsoft Chat.)
2. Select the Show All Available Chat Rooms option, and then click OK.

Choosing an Identity

1. Choose View, Options.
2. Choose the Personal Info tab, click in the Nickname box and then type a nickname for yourself.
3. Click the Character tab, and select the character you want to play.

Entering a Room

To enter a chat room, select a room from the chat room list.

Text Chatting

You can switch Chat into a "text mode" so it skips the comic characters and displays the conversation as scrolling series of text messages. To switch to text mode, choose View, Plain Text.

Joining a Chat

Now that you understand what chatting is all about, it's time to hit a server and see it for real. On the way, however, you'll perform some automatic configuration that Chat needs to operate properly.

Basic Survival

Opening Chat and Connecting to a Server

Before opening Microsoft Chat, you can be online or offline. If you're offline when you begin, Chat connects to the Internet automatically. Also, your browser need not be open for you to use Chat, although it won't hurt anything if it is open.

1. Open Chat. (In Windows 95/98, choose Programs, Internet Explorer, Microsoft Chat.) The Connect dialog box opens to let you choose a chat server.

2. Select the Show all available chat rooms option, and then click OK. After you're online, a list of all chat rooms available on the server appears. You are now connected to a chat server and ready to chat—except that, as a new user, you have not yet selected a nickname and a comic character, as described next.

Choosing an Identity

Before you can join in a chat, you must create a nickname. Because of Chat's unique presentation style, you must choose a comic character, too. In addition, you can optionally select a background that appears behind the characters in each panel of the comic, as you see it on your screen.

Before you begin, however, a word of caution: On the Personal Info tab (step 3 in the following list), you can enter other information besides your nickname, such as your real name and email address. Think carefully before doing so; whatever information you supply here can be seen by other members whose clients (like Chat) can display member profiles. If you want to keep your anonymity, enter your nickname and nothing else.

Chat remembers your identity for future sessions. You don't need to choose again, except to change it.

1. Choose View, Options. The Options dialog box appears.

2. Choose the Personal Info tab, if it is not already open.

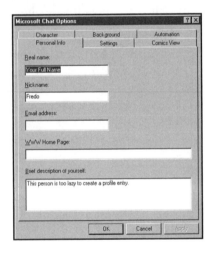

If you enter a room where someone is already using the same nickname as you, Chat prompts you to change your nickname.

3. Click in the Nickname box and type a nickname for yourself. Your nickname should be one word, using no spaces or punctuation, and it should also be unusual to reduce the chances that another member has chosen the same nickname.

4. Click the Character tab. This is where you select your character.

The Preview column shows what the character looks like—what you will look like to other Chat users.

5. Select the character you want to play by clicking a name in the Character column. Note that someone else in the chat may use the same character as you. Chatters can share characters, but not nicknames.

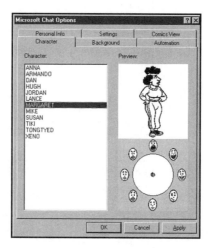

When you click a name in the Character column, you see the character in the Preview column.

6. Click the Background tab. This tab enables you to select from several cartoon backgrounds to use when chatting.

7. Choose a background. When you select an entry in the Background column, the background appears in the Preview column.

8. Click OK.

Entering a Room

To enter a chat room, select a room from the chat Room list. Each server has its own list, and the lists change often.

In the Room list, the name of each room begins with a hash mark (#). The name of the room is followed by the number of members currently in the room, and sometimes also by a description of the conversation that usually takes place there.

Open the Chat Room list any time you're connected to the server by clicking the Chat Room List button.

Understanding What You See

The Chat window is broken up into five sections, or panes (covered clockwise from upper left):

- The biggest pane is the viewing pane, where you see the chat session as it progresses.

- The small pane in the upper right is the member list pane, which lists all members in the current chat room.

- The pane showing your character is the self-view pane, which reminds you of who you are.

- The ring of faces is the emotion wheel, from which you can select your character's facial expression.

- The small text box at the bottom of the window is the compose pane, where you type your statements.

Member list pane

Viewing pane

Self-view pane

Emotion wheel

Compose pane

When you first arrive in a room, you may not see any comic panels right away. The server shows you only what's been said since you entered the room. After you enter, statements begin appearing, one by one, as members make them.

Beyond Survival

Text Chatting

You can switch Chat into a "text mode" so it skips the comic characters and displays the conversation as a scrolling series of text messages, like any other IRC client.

When the room is crowded (five or more members), you may prefer chatting in text mode. First, text chatting may make it easier to follow a crowded talk, because more messages can be seen onscreen at once than in Comics mode. Also, text chatting may speed up your PC's performance when you're chatting.

To switch to text mode, choose View, Plain Text. To switch back from text mode to comics, choose View, Comic Strip. You can switch back and forth at any time, even in the middle of a conversation.

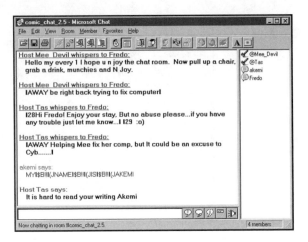

Cheat Sheet

Contributing to a Chat

When in a chat and ready to speak, simply begin typing. Anything you type while in a chat room appears automatically in the compose pane, the text box at the bottom of the Chat window.

As you type, you can use the Backspace, Delete, Insert, and arrow keys to edit your statement and correct mistakes. When the statement reads as you want it to, press Enter to send it to the chat.

Choosing Balloons

You can choose the style of the comic word balloon in which your words appear. Before pressing Enter to send your statement, click the desired balloon style button from the row to the right of the compose pane.

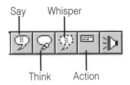

Showing Emotions

You can choose the emotion on the face of your character. Before pressing Enter to send your statement, click the desired facial expression on the emotion wheel.

Gesturing

Your character's gestures are selected automatically by Chat, based on words you use in your statements. For example, if a statement contains the word *I*, when speaking that statement your character appears to point to himself or herself. You can control gestures by wording your statements accordingly.

32

Contributing to a Chat

When you are in a chat room, you can just *lurk* (listen in) to the conversation, or you can contribute to it by sending your statements for all others to see. Lurking in a chat room is a great way to learn more about chats before diving in. But when you're ready to speak up, here's how...

Basic Survival

About Balloon Choices

When you contribute, you can choose the style of the comic word balloon in which your words appear to you and to other Chat users. You choose the style of the word balloon by clicking a button next to the compose pane, which is the text box at the bottom of the Chat window in which you type all your statements.

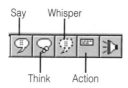

Say   Whisper

Think   Action

When you don't select a balloon style, the Say balloon is used by default.

For example, for a particular statement, you can choose a think balloon so the words appear in the balloon style generally used in comics to represent what the character is thinking. (Snoopy, for example, can't actually speak, so all of his words appear in thought balloons.)

Adding Your Two Cents

As you begin contributing to chats, keep in mind that while you're typing and editing your statements, no one sees them but you. A statement is sent to the chat only when you press Enter. That gives you a chance to choose your words carefully and correct typos before committing your statement to the chat.

1. Enter a chat room that interests you, and follow the conversation until you understand what's being talked about.

2. When you are ready to contribute, begin typing. Anything you type while in a chat room appears automatically in the compose pane, the text box at the bottom of the Chat window.

   As you type, you can use the Backspace, Delete, Insert, and arrow keys to edit your statement and correct mistakes.

Chat automatically gives your character certain gestures based on words in the statement (see the "Beyond Survival" section).

3. When your statement is worded the way you want, press Enter. After a few moments, your statement appears as part of the scrolling conversation displayed in the chat window.

   Those in the room using regular chat clients see your statement labeled with your nickname, so they know you said it. Those in the room using Microsoft Chat see your chosen comic character speaking the words in a *say balloon,* the type that surrounds words that comic characters say aloud.

4. Type a statement that's more a thought than a statement—an opinion, perhaps. Before pressing Enter to submit the statement, click the Think button in the compose pane; then press Enter. Chat users see your character thinking the words in a thought balloon.

5. Now think of a statement your character might whisper, rather than say aloud. Type the statement, click the Whisper button, and then press Enter. Chat users see your character whispering the words in the type of balloon that surrounds the whispers of comic characters.

Beyond Survival

Showing Emotions

The emotion wheel in the lower-right corner of the chat window lets you change the expression of your character's face when making a statement.

To use emotions, type your statement, but don't press Enter right away to send it. First, select a face from the emotion wheel. The character in the self-view pane changes to show how your character will appear if you commit to using the selected expression. As long as you don't press Enter, you can choose a different expression until you find one you like.

When the self-view pane appears the way you want it to, press Enter to submit your statement.

Some members may not be use Chat and can't see expressions, so be sure your words alone carry your meaning.

Gesturing

If you watch a chat for awhile, you'll notice that the characters are not static. They change body position and gestures, panel to panel.

To choose your character's normal, neutral expression, click the + at the center of the emotion wheel.

This gesturing is selected automatically by Chat, based on words you use in your statements. For example, if a statement contains the word *I*, your character appears to point to himself or herself. You can thus control gestures by wording your statements accordingly.

You can use other members' nicknames to control to whom the gesture is made. For example, if you say "Hi," your character appears to wave to the group. If you say "Hi, Eloise," your character appears to wave at the member using the nickname Eloise.

Some gestures are based on words used to begin a statement and others are based on words within the statement.

Gestures Used Automatically by Chat Characters

Statement Begins With	Character's Action
I	Points to itself
You	Points to another member
Hello or Hi	Waves
Bye	Waves
Welcome	Waves
Howdy	Waves

continues

Continued

If a statement begins with a gesture word and also has a gesture word within, Chat gestures based on the beginning word.

Statement Contains	Character's Action
are you	Points to another member
will you	Points to another member
did you	Points to another member
aren't you	Points to another member
don't you	Points to another member
I'm	Points to itself
I am	Points to itself
I'll	Points to itself
I will	Points to itself

PART

9

Making the Most of the Internet

Well, by now you've already discovered all the major online activities. So in this part, you won't pick up new skills so much as you'll learn how to do more with the skills you already possess, such as

- Finding Safe Family Fun
- Tips for Parents
- Shopping Online
- Selling Online

Cheat Sheet

Choosing a Family Starting Point

A good general-purpose family page provides a jumping off point from which all the links are family-friendly. Kids starting out should be taught to begin at that page, and use only the links on that page. A few good choices are

- Yahooligans! (www.yahooligans.com)
- 4Kids Treehouse (www.4kids.com)

Important Family Safety Steps

To help keep your family safe online, always

- Supervise your kids when they're online.
- Don't use features that permit anyone to use the Net without a password.
- Don't let your kids use chat, whether supervised or not.

Online Rules for Kids

Tell your kids

- Never reveal to anyone online your real name or any other identifying information.
- Never reveal anything about your parents, siblings, teachers, or friends.
- Never arrange to meet an online friend in person without a parent's involvement at every step.
- Never download or upload a file, or install any software on the computer, without a parent's okay.
- *Always* assume that people you meet online may *not* be who they say they are.

33

Find Safe Family Fun

Is cyberspace a family place? One day, the media touts the Net as the greatest thing since Gutenberg; the next, it's the harbinger of the Apocalypse, an instrument of pornographers, pedophiles, and disgruntled loners.

Actually, it's neither—it's just a tool. And like any tool, it can be put to good uses and bad. I think an adult has a right to use the Internet any way he or she wants to—within the law and without bothering anybody. But if you have kids who will use the Net (and they should!), you need to know how to insulate them from the Net's racier regions. In this chapter and the one that follows it, you learn common-sense rules for creep-proofing your kids (just in case you have some).

Basic Survival

Choosing a Family Starting Point

A good first step for family Web surfing is to choose a good starting point, a "family home page" of sorts.

A good general-purpose family page provides a jumping off point from which all the links are family-friendly. Kids starting out should be taught to begin at that page, use only the links on that page, and to use Back to return to that page after visiting any of its links. That habit corrals a kid's surfing to a limited, appropriate range of sites.

You may choose to make one of these family pages into your browser's regular home page (see Chapter 7, "Surfing Straight to a Web Site").

You'll probably want to browse and search for a family page that best fits your family (some good choices appear in Appendix A, "More Great Sites to Visit"), but here are a few suggestions:

- Yahooligans! (www.yahooligans.com). Kids offshoot of the Yahoo! search tool containing links and a search engine that both lead only to good kid stuff.

- 4Kids Treehouse (www.4kids.com). A colorful site with great links and activities for kids, plus resources for parents.

- Family.com (`www.family.com`). An online family magazine.

- Kids Avenue (`kidsavenue.home.mindspring.com`). A fun collection of kids links and activities.

- The American Library Association's Cool Sites for Kids page (`www.ala.org/alsc/children_links.html`). Contains links to book recommendations, kids' writings, homework help, games, and more.

After learning to create Web pages (Part 10, "Your Very Own Web Page"), you can create your own family page filled with links to good kid sites.

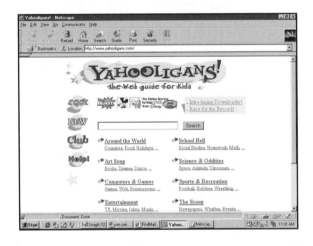

Important Family Safety Steps

To check where your unsupervised kid surfs, open the browser's history file (see Chapter 9, "Getting Back to Places You Like").

Everybody's different, and so is every family. It's not my place to say what's best for you or your kids. But in case you want some guidance about keeping your kids safe online, permit me to offer a few suggestions here. Then follow your own judgment.

Supervise!

This one's so obvious, and so difficult. As a parent I know that it isn't practical to supervise our kids every second of the day. To a tired parent of a preteen, the idea of the kid going off to his room for an hour to surf the Net is appealing.

You must make your own choice about when to cut the cord, based not on what's convenient, but on your kid. Some kids are mature enough to surf responsibly at 7, others can't be trusted at 17. Only you know your kids.

If you're not sure whether your kid is ready to go solo, but you don't have time to supervise, keep him offline until either he's ready or you have the time. The Internet has a lot to offer a kid, but your kid can live without it until the time is right for both of you.

Don't Defeat Passwords

Your Internet connection, email account, and a few other activities require you to enter a username and password, to prevent unauthorized access.

Some software, particularly Internet connection programs, enables you to enter the password in a dialog box once, so you never have to type it again. That's a convenient feature, but it enables anyone who can flip a switch to use your computer to get online.

If you think your password has been discovered, contact your Internet provider to change it.

My advice is that you leave your computer configured so a password is required for both connecting to the Internet and retrieving email. Never tell your kids the passwords, and never log on or retrieve email in their sight. That ensures that you always know when your kids are online, and that they cannot receive email from anyone without your knowledge.

Resist Chat

It's a shame, because there's plenty of good clean fun to be had in chat rooms. But it must be said: Chat's the most dangerous place on the Internet. That's not because of all the sex-related chat rooms, although it's related to those.

On the Web, the worst thing that can happen to a kid is that he or she gets exposed to ideas—words and pictures—you don't approve of. In chat, your kids can easily meet up with people who may hurt them. People are much more dangerous than ideas.

If you don't use chat yourself, don't install a chat client—then you needn't worry.

It works like this: A pedophile or other dangerous character—often posing as a kid—frequents chat rooms where kids hang out, and there establishes friendships, especially with lonely kids who are easy prey. As the friendship grows, the creep manipulates the kid into dropping the anonymous chat nicknames and exchanging email addresses, for private correspondence. Eventually, a private, face-to-face meeting is arranged. There already have been numerous cases of kids abused this way. The initial contact is almost always made in a chat room.

Obviously, I recommend never allowing a child to use chat unsupervised, even if that child is trusted to surf the Web unsupervised. But even supervised chatting is risky—by teaching a child how to chat, you increase the chances that the child may sneak a chat session unsupervised.

Beyond Survival

Online Rules for Kids

I know, my kids hate rules too. But these are pretty easy, and it's essential that you teach your kids these rules, even if you can't always be sure the rules will be followed.

In particular, if you have older kids you will permit to use the Net unsupervised, it's important that they know the rules for safe surfing.

Tell your kids:

- Never reveal to anyone online your real name, email address, phone number, mailing address, school name, or username/password without a parent's involvement and consent. Any other personal information, such as birthday or Social Security number, is also best kept secret. Never, ever, ever send anyone a picture of yourself.

Some suggest having the kids sign these rules as a contract, then hanging the contract above the computer.

- Never reveal anything about your parents, siblings, teachers, or friends. Any such information can help a creep find you, and exposes family and friends to risks, too.

- Never arrange to meet in person any online friend unless a parent consents before the meeting is arranged, the parent is present at that meeting, and that meeting takes place in a public setting, such as a restaurant or mall.

- Anytime you come across anything online that makes you uneasy, go elsewhere, or get offline. There's too much good stuff online to waste time looking at the bad.

- Never download or upload a file, or install any software on the computer, without a parent's okay.

- *Always* assume the people you meet online may *not* be who they say they are. Imposters pose as all kinds of people to rope in victims. Adult criminals often pose as kids to get the trust of their intended victims.

Cheat Sheet

Resources for Parents

You'll find plenty of parenting and safe surfing advice online, in places such as

- Parent Soup: www.parentsoup.com
- The Parents Place: www.parentsplace.com

Censoring Web Content

A variety of Internet-censoring programs are designed to filter out undesirable content. They work, but not without significant drawbacks.

Using Internet Explorer's Built-In Content Advisor

Internet Explorer has its own built-in system, Content Advisor, for controlling access to Web sites and chat rooms. You can enable Content Advisor by choosing View, Internet Options, Content, clicking the Enable button, and following the prompts.

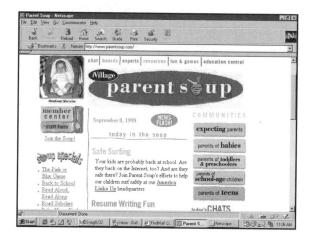

34

Tips for Parents

In Chapter 33, "Find Safe Family Fun," you learned the basics
of teaching your kids (if you have any) responsible surfing. It's
time to delve a little farther into stuff that's for parent's eyes
only (*shhhhh!*). The ideas in this chapter can help you make
your family Internet activities even safer, and more productive.

Basic Survival

Resources for Parents

Want to know more about protecting your kids online, teaching them to use the Net smartly, finding great family sites, or
just plain old parenting advice? You'll find all of this and more
online. Check out

- Parent Soup (www.parentsoup.com)

- The Parents Place (www.parentsplace.com)

- Kids Health (www.kidshealth.org)

- All About Kids magazine (www2.aak.com/aak)

Censoring Web Content

You've probably heard that there are programs that can control what your kids see online. So why didn't I just mention those in the first place, and save you all this "online rules" crud in Chapter 33?

Well, it's debatable how effective these programs are. First, most are really focused on the Web, and often aren't much protection elsewhere, such as chat or email. Most censoring programs—erring properly on the cautious side, I suppose—inevitably censor out totally benign stuff that you or your kids may find valuable.

If you super-vise kids online—and you should—you don't need a censoring program.

Also, these programs may filter out sexual content, depictions of violence, and profanity. But what about ugly ideas? For example, the programs generally do not block out racist, sexist, or nationalist hatemongering, as long as those views are expressed without the use of profanity or epithets. Even though these self-censoring tools are available, they're no replacement for supervision.

Getting a Safe-Surfing Program

Microsoft Internet Explorer has its own censoring program, which you'll learn about next. If you don't use Internet Explorer, or if you do but don't like Content Advisor, you'll want to check out the Web pages of other popular self-censoring utilities.

From these pages, you can learn more about each product, and in most cases, download a copy for your system:

- Net Nanny (www.netnanny.com)
- SurfWatch (www.surfwatch.com)
- Cybersitter (www.solidoak.com/cysitter.htm)
- The Internet Filter (turnercom.com/if)
- CyberPatrol (www.cyberpatrol.com)

Beyond Survival

**Using IE's
Content
Advisor**

Internet Explorer (versions 3 and 4) has its own built-in system, Content Advisor, for controlling access to Web sites and chat rooms. Content Advisor works much like the other safe-surfing programs (except it's a little harder to use than some), and it possesses many of the same strengths and drawbacks.

**How Does
It Work?**

Content Advisor works by relying on a rating system from the Recreational Software Advisory Council (RSAC), which also rates entertainment software and video games. The RCSA ratings system assigns a score (0–4) to a Web site or chat room for each of four criteria: Language, Nudity, Sex, and Violence. The higher the score in each category, the more intense the content that page or room contains.

For example, if a site has a score of 0 in the Language category, it contains nothing worse than "inoffensive slang." A Language score of 4, however, indicates "explicit or crude language" on the site. When a Web site has been rated, the rating is built in to the site, so Content Advisor can read the page's score before displaying anything.

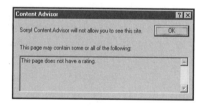

You can choose an option that allows unrated pages, but doing so defeats the purpose of Content Advisor.

There's one problem: Only a tiny portion of sites online have been rated. Enabling Content Advisor, therefore, blocks not only rated pages you might find offensive but also *all* pages—offensive or not—that have not been rated, which means most of the Web.

As you may guess, blocking unrated pages severely cramps your surfing and has little to do with protecting you from offensive content.

Enabling Content Advisor

If you choose to try Content Advisor, here's how. (You needn't be online to do this.)

1. In Internet Explorer, open the Internet Options dialog box (choose View, Internet Options), then choose the Content tab.

2. In the tab's Content Advisor section, click the Enable button. A dialog box opens, prompting for your Supervisor password.

3. Type a password, and then press Tab to jump down to the Confirm Password box. Type your password again, and then press Enter. The Ratings tab of the Content Advisor dialog box opens.

To disable Content Advisor later, repeat step 1, then click the Disable button on the Content tab.

The Supervisor password prevents others from disabling Content Advisor or changing the settings.

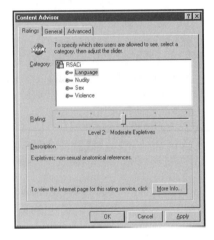

The farther right you pull the slider, the more lenient the setting. Think that 0 = a G rating, 1 = PG, 2 = PG-13, and so on.

4. Click the Language category. The Rating scale shows the current setting for Language.

5. Point to the slider (the rectangle) on the Rating scale, click and hold, and drag the slider along the scale. As the slider reaches each marker on the scale, a description appears below the scale, telling what type of language that setting permits.

6. Release the slider at your preferred setting for Language.

7. Repeat steps 4, 5, and 6 for each of the other three categories: Nudity, Sex, and Violence.

8. When you have finished choosing ratings, click the General tab. On the General tab, you can selectively check or uncheck the check box for two important options:

- **Users can see sites that have no rating.** Check this check box to allow the display of unrated pages. Content Advisor continues to block rated pages that exceed your settings but permits unrated pages, regardless of their content.

- **Supervisor can type a password to allow users to see restricted content.** When this check box is checked, when someone tries to open a page Content Advisor would block, a dialog box pops up, prompting for the Supervisor password. If the password is typed, the page appears.

9. After selecting your options on the General tab, click OK. Content Advisor is enabled, and the Content tab of the Internet Options dialog box reappears.

The password option allows kids to appeal to you for a temporary censorship waiver for a particular Web site.

Cheat Sheet

Shopping 'til You Drop

Using only the Web-surfing skills you already possess (such as filling in forms), you can enjoy the benefits of online shopping, such as

- 24-hour, 365-day shopping
- Access to product photos and specifications
- Web specials and discounts
- Custom ordering options

Making an online purchase usually requires typing your credit card number and other sensitive information in a form, so never buy from an unsecured site (review Chapter 10, "Protecting Your Privacy").

Using Accounts and Shopping Baskets

Many merchants equip their storefronts with either or both of the following to make shopping there more convenient:

- Accounts keep your name, payment information, and shipping address on file with the online merchant to make future orders easier.
- Shopping baskets let you conveniently choose multiple products, then place the order for everything at once, instead of having to order each item as you select it.

Buying Stocks and Such

The Web is a great place to sell intangible goods, such as stocks or securities. Such purchases carry the greatest risk among online shopping activities because they involve moving around large amounts of money, putting it at risk in investments, and revealing detailed personal information about yourself (such as your Social Security number). The steps for online investing are roughly the same as those buying anything else online.

35

Shopping Online

Feel the need to spend? In this chapter, you'll expand upon what you picked up in Chapters 10 and 11 (filling in forms, using security) by learning how to shop and invest online—safely.

Basic Survival

Shopping 'til You Drop

Whattaya wanna buy? Whatever it is, you can probably buy it from a virtual storefront on a Web page.

Using only the Web-surfing skills you already possess, you can enjoy the benefits of online shopping:

- **24-hour, 365-day shopping.** Except for rare moments when the server is down for maintenance and repair, online stores are always open, like many Denny's or Wal-Marts.

- **Access to product photos and specifications.** While browsing an online catalog, you often can click links to display product photos, lists of options, and even detailed measurements or other specifications. Such is the stuff of an informed buying decision.

Sites with lots of products may include a search tool you can use to find products or types of product.

- **Web specials.** Some merchants offer discounts or other deals that are available only to those ordering online, and not to phone, mail order, or in-person customers.

- **Custom ordering.** Some stores feature forms that let you specify exactly what you want. For example, PC sellers online such as Dell or Gateway let you choose each specification of a PC—processor, hard disk size, CD-ROM speed, and so on—from lists in a form. When you finish, the price for your system appears, along with a link for placing the order.

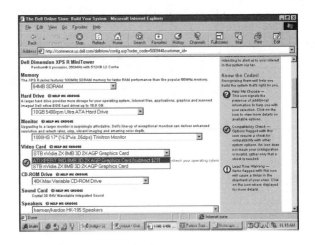

Is Shopping Online Safe?

You know this already, but it bears repeating: Making an online purchase usually requires typing your credit card number and other sensitive information in a form. That's something you should never do on a site that's not secure (review Chapter 10).

Explore virtual storefronts to your heart's content, comparing prices and other terms to make the best buy. But upon arriving at the page where you fill in your order form or open an account with the merchant, confirm that the page on which the form appears is secure. If the order form is not on a secure page, buy elsewhere.

In most browsers, a secure site is indicated by a locked padlock icon or unbroken gold key near the bottom of the window.

Even on a secure site, caveat emptor (buyer beware). A secure site protects you from being scammed by a third party, but doesn't protect you if the owner of the site is a cheat.

As an online consumer, it is in your best interest to be informed. You can find reviews of products and merchants all over the Web; one good way to find reviews is to use the product name and the word "review" together as a search term. You may also want to check out the Web pages of consumer advocates, who help us beware by alerting us to schemes, scams, and duds:

- Consumer's Union (publishers of *Consumer Reports* magazine): www.ConsumerReports.org

- Consumer World: www.consumerworld.org

Using Accounts and Shopping Baskets

You already know how to fill out a form, and usually that's all there is to shopping. But many merchants equip their storefronts with either or both of the following to make shopping there more convenient:

- Accounts. When you set up an account with an online merchant, you give that merchant a record of your name and shipping address, and often your credit card information, too. After entering this information once, you can shop and buy anytime without having to enter it again. All you have to do is enter an account username and password, and the site knows who you are, how you pay, and where to ship your stuff.

- Shopping baskets. A shopping basket lets you conveniently choose multiple products, then place the order for everything at once, instead of having to order each item as you select it. Shopping baskets also provide you with a chance to look over your list of selections, and the total price, so you can change or delete items before committing to the order.

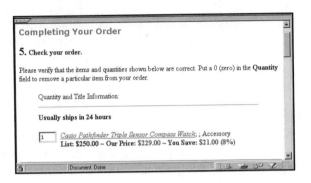

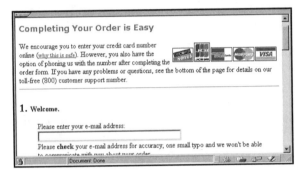

Beyond Survival

Buying Stocks and Such

The Web is a great place to sell intangible goods, such as stocks or securities—after all, if the product is intangible, why shouldn't the transaction be?

Obviously, such purchases carry the greatest risk among online shopping activities. They generally involve moving around large amounts of money, and putting it at risk in investments. But if that's your thing, you should know that trading online can be substantially cheaper than using a traditional broker, and in many cases your transactions are executed much more quickly, usually within minutes.

The steps for online investing are roughly the same as those for buying anything else online. Typically, you set up an account with an online brokerage, after which you may buy and sell at will.

Opening an account with an online broker typically requires disclosing detailed information about yourself; you'll have to disclose your bank account numbers, Social Security number, and other private, sensitive information you would not have to reveal when making other kinds of online purchases.

Investment Starting Points

To learn more about investing online, or to take the plunge and buy that 1,000 shares of Yugo, consult the sites in the sections that follow.

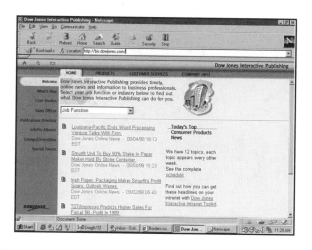

For Financial Information and Advice

To learn more about online investing, read company profiles, and explore other money matters, check out:

- CNN's Financial News Network: cnnfn.com

- *Wall Street Journal*: www.wsj.com

- Dow Jones Business Information Services: bis.dowjones.com

- MoneyAdvisor: www.moneyadvisor.com

- *Success* Magazine: www.successmagazine.com

- Yahoo! Finance: `quote.yahoo.com`

- Finance Online: `www.finance-online.com`

- American Stock Exchange: `www.amex.com`

- NASDAQ: `www.nasdaq.com`

For Making Investments

If you're ready to go ahead and put your money on the line (online!), visit the online brokers:

- Mr. Stock: `www.mrstock.com`

- American Express Financial Services Direct: `www.americanexpress.com/direct`

- E*Trade: `www.etrade.com`

- Charles Schwab: `www.eschwab.com`

- Wall Street Electronica: `www.wallstreete.com`

Cheat Sheet

About a "Web Presence"

This term describes the online identity and means of accessibility for a company. An important first step in taking a business online is choosing your initial degree of presence, the extent to which your company does business online. Options include

- Virtual Storefront. A complete online catalog and ordering system, which requires the greatest commitment from the company.
- Informational/Advertising Page. A page that promotes the company and its products, but does not provide online ordering.

Your Own Domain

Sites such as www.toyota.com or www.kodak.com have their own Internet domains to identify their owners. If you set up and maintain your own Web server, you get your own domain along with it. If you use space on another's server but want your own domain, you can apply for the domain and pay a fee for it.

Publicizing Your Storefront

Within a month or so after you put your company online, most of the search tools will have found your page and added it to their databases. But to ensure that customers find you, you should also visit such tools as Yahoo! and Excite and manually add your page to their databases.

Besides adding your site to search tool databases, you can promote it through

- Print/broadcast advertising
- Company stationery
- Email signatures

Selling Online

36

If you're exploring taking your own business into cyberspace, or if you've been put in charge of exploring that option for your employer, you already know that your research must consist of more than one chapter in this book. But here is a good place for you to begin considering what your company's Web presence should be like.

Basic Survival

About a "Web Presence"

What's a "Web presence"? Sometimes also expressed as online presence, this term describes the online identity and means of accessibility for a company; a company with a Web page and email address has an online presence.

Beyond learning about your options for establishing a Web presence, you must also consider the laws and other issues related to expanding the scope of your business—online or offline.

Your business Web page makes you an interstate (even international) business, one that must follow regulations pertaining to collection of sales tax, currency conversions, truth in advertising, and other laws of interstate and international commerce. Today, most of these laws are the same as those you'd follow if you did interstate/international business by mail order or telephone, although in coming years a distinct set of rules governing online commerce will evolve.

To learn more about doing business online, check out

- The *Web Commerce Today* newsletter (www.wilsonweb.com/wct/)
- BizWeb (www.bizweb.com)
- AT&T's Business page (www.att.com/business)
- U.S. Small Business Administration (www.sbaonline.sba.gov)

Choosing a Degree of Presence

An important first step in taking a business online is choosing your initial degree of presence, the extent to which your company does business online. Many companies choose merely to promote themselves online, but don't actually sell there. Others are committed to offering online every product and service they have.

Each level of Web presence requires a different level of commitment and resources from the company, in the form of time, money, and personnel.

Take care to choose a degree of online presence that you or your company can keep up with. Many companies overreach in their early forays online, deploying elaborate Web sites that they fail to update regularly and keep working smoothly.

Virtual Storefront

This is the Holy Grail of Web presence, and for companies offering products or services that travel well, it's a great way to expand.

But a real virtual storefront—including a catalog and ordering system—also requires the greatest commitment from the company. Above and beyond the demands of creating a Web page—which anyone can do (see Chapter 37, "Understanding Web Page Authoring")—an online ordering system requires

- Programming. An ordering system requires scripts to process orders from what customers type in forms online. Writing those scripts demands programming experience and knowledge of a language such as Java, JavaScript, or CGI.

- Security. Processing orders demands creating and maintaining a secure Web site, which takes the skills of a dedicated, full-time administrator. To ensure maximum security for transactions, most companies own and operate their own Web servers—which dramatically increases the cost of a Web presence.

- Customer Service. A script can process orders, but dealing with customer questions and complaints requires experienced customer service personnel whom customers

Programmers with Java and CGI skills are in high demand, so they rarely come cheap (if they're good).

can contact via email or phone. Too often, companies expect existing personnel to also service Web customers, forcing Web customers to wait days or weeks for responses to queries. That's bad e-business.

• Professional Design. Sure, you can send some entry-level employee off in a corner with a computer and a Web authoring book, and he or she will manage to produce a Web page. But if you take a look at what your competition is doing, you may notice that companies seeking a professional-looking online identity hire highly skilled, professional Web designers.

Informational/Advertising Page

For companies just starting out online, a full ordering system is prohibitive, and unnecessary. Even today, most companies use the Web not to sell directly, but to promote themselves and to provide customers (or investors) with company and product information.

On such pages, you'll often find a toll-free telephone number for placing orders. This approach is a great first step for a company that has a telephone sales or mail order sales organization in place, but is not yet ready to create and maintain an effective online ordering system.

A promotional page such as this has another benefit: By offering Web discounts a customer can take when calling, the company can easily track the amount of business generated by the Web. This information is critical to evaluating whether and when the company should move up to a full virtual storefront.

Selling Online but Off-Web

Finally, it's worth noting that the Web is not the only medium for selling online.

A mailing list (see Chapter 24, "Subscribing to a Mailing List") can make an excellent sales tool. Many Internet programmers can set up and maintain a Listserv for you, which you can promote to customers through a simple Web page or your print

and mail advertising. Because customers have the power to subscribe to and unsubscribe from the list, you know that those on
the list at any given time are interested, well-qualified sales
leads.

As an alternative to a Listserv, you can broadcast email promo-
tions to thousands of customers. But as I hope the discussion of
spam in Chapter 23, "Stopping Junk Email," showed you,
sending unsolicited commercial email may win you more ene-
mies than buyers. Limit your bulk emailing to customers who
have explicitly expressed the desire to receive them. (Using a
Listserv can help you ensure this.)

Beyond Survival

**Your Own
Domain**

An increasingly important part of having a Web presence is
having one's own domain, a unique Internet server address
that identifies a company online. Sites such as www.toyota.com
or www.kodak.com have domains that identify—and thus
promote—their owners.

For example, I can set up a Web page on an ISP's server without getting my own domain. But my page's URL would be
something like

```
www.isp.com/users/nedsnell/index.html
```

The server
owner can
help you apply
for a domain
and pay the
fee, which
goes to
InterNIC,
the group in
charge of
domains.

If I buy a domain, I can be

```
www.nedsnell.com
```

which is much better for establishing a memorable online identity.

If you set up and maintain your own Web server, you get your
own domain along with it. If you use space on another's server
but want your own domain, you must apply for the domain
and pay a fee (usually $70 to create the domain and pay for the
first two years, then $35 per year thereafter).

Publicizing Your Storefront

After establishing a Web presence, you have to get the word out, to let everybody know that cyberspace is your space, too.

Within a month or so after you put your company online, most of the search tools based on crawlers (see Chapter 14, "Finding a Search Tool") will have found your page and added it to their databases. But to ensure that customers find you, you should also visit such tools as Yahoo! and Excite and manually add your page to their databases.

For example, to add your site to Yahoo! (www.yahoo.com), browse to the category in which you want your site listed, then click the How to Suggest a Site button at the bottom of the page. Follow the prompts, and you'll soon arrive at a form in which you can type your site's URL and descriptive information.

Besides adding your site to search tool databases, you can promote it through

- Print/broadcast advertising. Make sure your domain, Web site address, and email address appears prominently in all your ads. A growing number of companies even incorporate their site address in store signs and the company logo.

- Company stationery. Next time you print business cards or letterhead, add your URL. Put the Web site URL on all employee business cards, along with the employee's email address.

- Email. Most email programs let you create a signature, a boilerplate block of text added automatically to the bottom of every message you send. If you use a signature, you can include the Web site address in it.

PART 10

Your Very Own Web Page

Got something to say, or to sell? Want to offer your experiences or expertise to the world? There's no better way to do that today than by creating and publishing your own Web page.

Building a Web page is easier than you might think—if you know how to surf the Web and use any word processing program, you already possess the prerequisite skills for Web authoring. This part takes you the rest of the way, showing you several ways to create attractive Web pages. The basic skills you'll learn here form a foundation upon which you can build later, on your own, to add other, advanced techniques to your skillset. Here you'll explore

- Understanding Web Page Authoring
- Creating a Web Page
- Publishing Your Web Page
- Creating Fancy, Formatted Messages

Cheat Sheet

What's in a Web Page, Really?

A Web page is a file in a format called HTML. An HTML file contains nothing but text: The text you'll see online, and instructions for how that text is to appear. The text in an HTML file also describes the URLs where links lead, and the filenames, locations, and page positions of any pictures, which are stored in their own, separate files.

What Tools Can I Use to Write a Page?

Most Web pages today are written in WYSIWYG Web authoring programs, which show you the page as it will look online, while you're working on it. Full installations of the big Internet suites both include a free WYSIWYG authoring program:

- Communicator suite includes Page Composer.
- Internet Explorer 4 includes FrontPage Express.

Where Do I Get the Pictures?

The pictures you'll use in your Web pages can come from anywhere: You can draw them in a paint program, scan them from your own photos, or even use images captured by a digital camera. Before you can use picture files, however, they must be saved in (or converted to) one of the two image file types supported in Web pages: GIF (file extension .gif) or JPEG (file extension .jpg).

You can also download images from clip-art libraries available online and in commercial and shareware software packages.

37

Understanding Web Page Authoring

Before you can dive into creating a Web page, you need to pick up a more intimate understanding of how a Web page works than you get by surfing the Web.

Basic Survival

What's in a Web Page, Really?

A Web page is actually a file in a format called HTML. An HTML file contains nothing but text—the actual text you'll see online, and instructions for how that text is to appear. The text in an HTML file also includes the URLs where any links in the page lead, and the filenames, locations, and page positions of any pictures or other multimedia files, which are stored in their own, separate files.

When the file is viewed through the browser, the browser interprets the HTML instructions to display the fully formatted page.

When an HTML file is viewed through a Web browser, the browser interprets the instructions in the file. The browser formats the text onscreen as ordered, locates the picture files, and displays them in their specified positions. The browser also reads and remembers the URLs the links point to, so it knows where to take a visitor who clicks one.

One page can look slightly different through different browsers, because each browser interprets HTML a little differently.

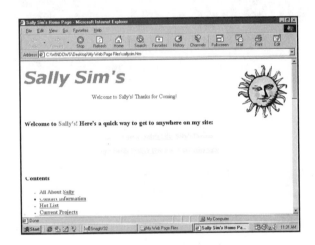

In general, the formatting instructions contained in an HTML file do not precisely control how the page appears. Rather, the file provides a general idea of how the page is to appear, and each browser realizes those instructions slightly differently.

Parts of a Page

A Web page can be made up of many different parts, but most Web pages contain most or all of the following core elements:

The real title doesn't show within the layout of the page, although many authors repeat the title in a big heading.

- **Title.** Browsers typically display the title in the title bar of the window in which the page appears.

- **Headings.** Browsers typically display headings in large, bold, or otherwise emphasized type. A Web page can have many headings, and headings can be nested up to six levels deep; that is, there can be subheadings, and sub-subheadings, and so on.

- **Normal text.** Makes up the basic, general-purpose text of the page.

- **Horizontal lines.** (Sometimes called "rules") which dress up the page and separate it into logical sections.

- Hyperlinks. (Or simply *links*) to many different things: other Web pages, multimedia files (external images, animation, sound, video), document files, and so on.

- Lists. Bulleted (like this one) or numbered.

- Inline images. Pictures that are incorporated into the layout of the page to jazz it up or make it more informative.

- Background. Inline image that, unlike a regular image, covers the entire background of the page so text and other images can be seen on top of it.

- Tables. Text and inline images organized in neat rows and columns.

Instead of an image, you can use a solid background color.

What Tools Can I Use to Write a Page?

If you were skilled in HTML code, you could write a Web page simply by typing the correct code in a text file, in any word processor, or in a text editing program (like Windows Notepad). Some folks do it that way, but doing so makes it hard to see what you're creating; you have to jump from the editor to a browser every time you want to see how the page will look online.

A better choice is a *WYSIWYG* Web authoring program. A WYSIWYG Web authoring program shows you the page as it will look online, while you're working on it.

WYSIWYG = What You See Is What You Get—as you work, you can see how the page will look online.

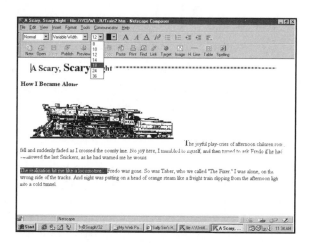

If you're careful to select and install the complete suite, you get a WYSIWYG editor with either of the Big Two Internet suites:

- The full Communicator suite includes Page Composer, which you open from within Navigator by choosing Communicator, Page Composer.

- The full Internet Explorer 4 suite includes FrontPage Express, which you open from the same menu where you can open the browser (in Windows 95, choose Programs, Internet Explorer, FrontPage Express).

Even when you use a WYSIWYG editor, your pages may look different in different browsers—WYS is not exactly WYG.

You can learn about other Web authoring programs by using a search tool (see Chapter 16, "Using Search Terms") to search for "Web authoring" or "HTML editor." You can also check out tucows.mcp.com.

Beyond Survival

Where Do I Get the Pictures?

The pictures you'll use in your Web pages can come from anywhere: You can draw them in a paint program (such as CorelDRAW! or Windows 95/98's Paint accessory), scan them from your own photos, or even use images captured by a digital camera.

What matters isn't the source of the pictures, but the image file format in which they're stored. The pictures you may include in a Web page either as inline images or as background images must be in either the GIF (.gif) or JPEG (.jpg) file format.

GIF is often best because all browsers support it, but JPEG is supported by most, and looks better when the picture is a photo.

If the program you use to create images won't save in GIF or JPEG format, many paint programs (and some Web authoring programs) can convert your files to GIF or JPEG.

When creating or editing images, keep in mind that the larger the file size of a picture, the longer it will take to travel through the Net to your visitors. Pages with large picture files (or with many different picture files) may take so long to show up that your visitors get impatient and split first. As a rule of thumb, try to keep the combined number of kilobytes (KB) in all pictures within one page under 100 for best performance.

You can often use your image-editing program to reduce the number of kilobytes in a picture by

- *Scaling* the picture so it appears smaller on the screen (which also makes it take up fewer bytes).

- Saving the picture at a reduced resolution; 75 *dpi* (dots per inch) is fine for Web graphics.

- Saving the picture with a reduced number of colors; saving a 256-color picture as a 16-color picture dramatically reduces the file size, and the picture may still look just as good (or nearly so).

When your picture isn't GIF, IE4's FrontPage Express lets you use it anyway, and automatically converts it to GIF.

Finally, if you want to use pictures, but don't want to create them, you can find libraries of commercial, shareware, and free clip art files in GIF and JPEG format at the software store and online.

When using clip art or any other picture you did not create yourself, be sure to read and obey any copyright restrictions on the Web site or other source from which you take the picture. And if you can't find any copyright notice there, don't use the picture—it may still be copyrighted, and you have no way of knowing the conditions under which you might be permitted to use it.

Some art online is in animated GIFs—pictures that move when used in a Web page. You use these exactly like ordinary GIFs.

Good online starting places for getting clip art (and other media, such as sounds) include

- Macmillan Computer Publishing's Design Resources Page (www.mcp.com/resources/design)

- Free Graphics (www.jgpublish.com/free.htm)

- Clip Art Universe (www.nzwwa.com/mirror/clipart/)

- WebSpice (www.webspice.com)

- Multimedia/Clip Art Directory (www.clipart.com/)

Cheat Sheet

Making Quick Pages with a Wizard

The quickest way to build a page is by running a Page Wizard. Both Composer and FrontPage Express have one of these wizards, which lead you through filling in a few quick dialog boxes and choosing some options.

Composing a Page in a WYSIWYG Editor

Composing a Web page in a WYSIWYG editor is much like composing and formatting a document in any word processor. You type your text, and format it by selecting it with your mouse and applying formatting—such as bold, fonts, and so on—from toolbar buttons or menu items.

Using Your Word Processor to Create a Web Page

Many word processors (such as recent versions of Word or WordPerfect), desktop publishing programs (such as Microsoft Publisher 98), and just about any other program that creates a document can optionally save files in HTML format, making that program's creations into Web page files that can be published online or edited and enhanced in your WYSIWYG editor.

38

Creating a Web Page

Now that you understand what a Web page is really made of, it's time to discover how easily you can create your own Web page.

Basic Survival

Making Quick Pages with a Wizard

The quickest way to build a page is by running a Page Wizard. Both Composer and FrontPage Express have one of these wizards, which leads you through filling in a few quick dialog boxes and choosing some options. When you finish, the wizard spits out a finished page, ready for publishing.

A wizard doesn't give you as much control as composing the page in a Web authoring program. But using a wizard is faster, and if the results aren't exactly what you want, you can always open your wizard-built page in your Web authoring program and edit it to change whatever you want to.

If you have IE4's FrontPage Express, try its wizard (which works offline) by choosing File, New, Personal Home Page.

If you have Netscape Communicator, you can practice using Page Composer's Wizard by following these steps. Note that Page Composer's Wizard is unusual because you must use it online.

1. Open Navigator (not Composer) and connect to the Internet.

2. In Navigator, choose File, New, Page From Wizard. This instructs the browser to connect to the Page Wizard page at

   `home.netscape.com/home/gold4.0_wizard.html`

   The wizard page is split into three frames:

   • Instructions. The upper-left frame describes each element you will create. Within each description are links that, when clicked, display a form or list of choices in the bottom frame.

- Choices. The bottom frame is where you will type text in forms (to create page content) or choose aspects of the look of your page from lists of choices.

- Preview. The upper-right frame shows a preview of your page as you develop it.

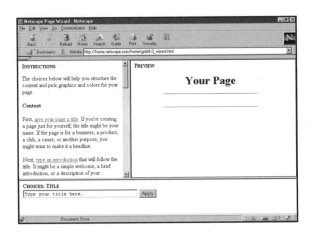

3. In the active frame (upper right), scroll down past Netscape's cheery introductory copy to display the Start button, and click it.

4. Scroll the Instructions frame until you see the link to give your page a title, and click that link. A form appears in the Choices frame. Delete the text that appears in the form and type a title for your page.

The wizard uses the title you type in step 4 as the HTML document title and as a large, bold heading atop the page.

5. Click Apply. The new title appears in the Preview frame, centered at the top of the page.

6. Scroll down the Instructions until you see another link to a page element you can create. Click it, then follow the instructions to complete the form in the bottom frame.

Continue defining page elements until the Preview frame shows a page to your liking. (Note that you can scroll the Instructions backward at any time to make changes.)

7. When done, scroll to the bottom of the Instructions frame, where you will see buttons labeled Build and Start Over.

8. Click Build. The finished page opens in Navigator.

9. From Navigator's menu bar, choose File, Edit Page. Composer opens, displaying your new home page.

The page is named Yourpage.html, which you can change, but make sure the file extension remains .htm or .html.

10. Click the Save button on Composer's toolbar (or choose File, Save As), select a folder and file name for your page, and save it.

11. Click Save to save the file. Your page is ready to be published or to be edited further in your Web authoring program.

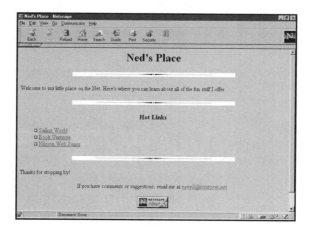

Beyond Survival

Composing a Page in a WYSIWYG Editor

Composing a Web page in a WYSIWYG editor is much like composing and formatting a document in any word processor. You type your text and then format it by selecting it with your mouse and applying formatting—such as bold, fonts, and so on—from toolbar buttons or menu items.

If you look at the toolbars in FrontPage Express or Composer, you'll probably recognize many of the tools, such as a drop-down list for choosing a font or a big B button for applying Bold.

It's the style you assign to text that really tells browsers how to handle it.

Although the Web authoring programs present you with lots of formatting tools, it bears repeating here that precise formatting you apply—such as font selections—may not be supported by all browsers through which your work may be seen. The formatting that matters most is the application of styles, which you choose in both Composer or FrontPage Express from a drop-down list on the toolbar.

FrontPage Express starts a new page whenever you open it, but you can also start one by choosing File, New, Normal Page.

If you have FrontPage Express (in Internet Explorer 4), try the following steps to practice creating a Web page:

1. Open FrontPage Express by choosing Programs, Internet Explorer, FrontPage Express from the Windows Start menu.

2. From the menu bar, choose File, Page Properties. The Page Properties dialog box opens.

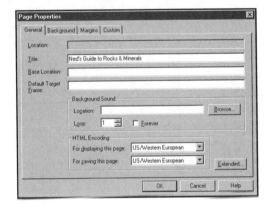

3. Click the General tab if it is not already selected, and then click in the Title box.

To learn the name of any button or list on the toolbar, point to it and wait a beat—its name appears.

4. Delete the automatic title, and type one of your own. Then click OK to close the dialog box.

5. Right after giving your page a title is a good time to save it for the first time. Click the Save button in the toolbar or choose File, Save. A special Save dialog box opens.

6. In the dialog box, click the As File button.

After the first time you save, you can save the file at any time just by clicking the Save button on the toolbar.

To select text, click and hold before it, drag to highlight, and then release.

Before adding a picture, copy the picture file into the same folder as the Web page HTML file.

Move a picture by dragging it where you want it. Resize it by dragging its borders.

7. Choose a folder for the page file, and type a name for the file in the File name box. Then click the Save button to save the file.

8. Now type and edit the text of your page, just as you would in any word processor. Don't worry yet about formatting that text; just get the words down.

9. After your text is typed, you may format the text. Begin by selecting a paragraph to format.

10. Click the Change Style drop-down list from the toolbar, and choose a style (Normal, a heading, and so on) to apply to the selected text.

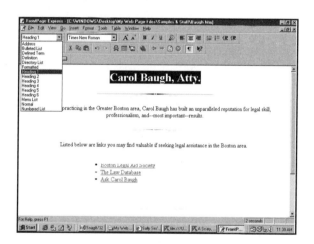

11. Now add a picture, if you happen to have an image file. The file should be in GIF or JPEG format, but if it isn't, use it anyway—FrontPage Express can probably convert it for you.

In the page, click at the general spot within the text where you want the picture to go. Then click the Insert Image button on the toolbar.

12. Click Browse to browse for and select the image file.

13. Now add a background. Open the Page Properties dialog box (choose File, Page Properties) and click the Background tab.

To create an image background, select the Background Image check box, and then click Browse to browse for and select a GIF image file, just as you would when inserting a picture.

To create a color background, choose a color from the Background drop-down list.

14. Finally, add a link. Begin by selecting the text that will serve as the link.

15. Click the Create or Edit Hyperlink button on the tool bar. The Create Hyperlink dialog box opens.

    When you're creating a link to another Web page, the Hyperlink Type box should read http://. If not, drop down the list and choose http://, which is the required type for a Web page. (Note, however, that the list lets you create links to resources other than Web pages, such as a link to your email address.)

16. In the URL box, type the URL of the Web page to which this link should lead when clicked by a visitor. Be sure to leave the http:// prefix on the URL. Click OK to create the URL.

17. Save your page one last time. Now it's ready for publishing (see Chapter 39, "Publishing Your Web Page"), or further editing and refinement.

Using Your Word Processor to Create a Web Page

Besides using a Web authoring program or a wizard, there's one more way to create a page: your word processor or desktop publishing program.

Increasingly, word processors (such as recent versions of Word or WordPerfect), desktop publishing programs (such as Microsoft Publisher 98), and just about any other program that creates a document can optionally save files in HTML format.

A word processor is not as good for authoring as a real Web authoring program, but it will do in a pinch. More important, these programs make it easy for you to convert existing documents into Web page files. For example, you can open your resume in Word, then save it as an HTML file—now it's ready for the Web.

Word 97 has a wizard for making new Web pages. Choose File, New, click the Web Pages tab, and then choose the Web Page Wizard icon.

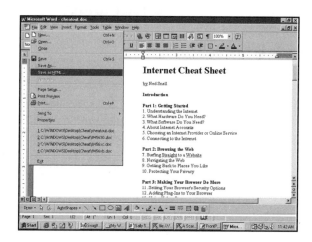

Cheat Sheet

Where to Publish?

To publish, you need space on somebody's Web server—enough to hold all the files that make up your page. You may be able to get permission to publish on your company's or school's server; otherwise, you need to acquire space on another server, usually your Internet provider.

You need to know the following information about the server:

- The server's address.
- The *uploading protocol* used by the server.
- Any username and password that you are required to use to gain access to the server.
- The directory in which your files will be stored.

Using a Publishing Utility

You can make uploading easier by supplying those instructions to a Web publishing program like those built into FrontPage Express and Composer.

Using FTP to Publish

Some folks find uploading their Web pages to a server easiest with an Internet tool called an FTP client. Windows 95 and the Mac have their own built-in FTP clients, but these are difficult for beginners. A better choice is an easy-to-use graphical FTP client, which combines the simplicity of a Web browser with the full power of FTP.

39

Publishing Your Web Page

After your Web page is finished, you must copy it to a Web server so others on the Internet can see it. That's *Web publishing*—and here's how to make it happen.

Basic Survival

Where to Publish?

Before you can publish, you need space on somebody's Web server—enough to hold all the files that make up your page (the HTML file plus any picture files).

Most Internet providers give their customers a megabyte or two of free server space—more than enough for several pages.

A typical Web page with a picture or two usually requires less than 100KB (kilobytes) of space on a server. The larger and more picture-laden your page, the more server space you'll need. The following are a few suggestions for finding a place to publish:

- If your page is related to your job, you may be able to get permission to publish it on your company's server; talk to your company's network administrator or Webmaster.

- Most colleges and universities also have Web servers and often allow students and faculty to publish on them.

- If you don't have permission to publish your Web page on your company's or school's server and don't plan to create your own server (which is prohibitively expensive and technical for beginners), you need to acquire space on somebody else's Web server, usually your Internet provider's Web server.

After you know whose server will hold your Web page files, you must upload the files from your PC to the server. The exact procedures for doing this differ by server or Internet provider; you must get complete uploading instructions directly from the company whose server you will use.

Uploading = copying files from your computer to a server—the opposite of downloading.

Many Internet providers summarize their uploading procedures on their Web page.

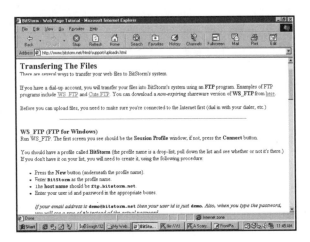

If you publish on your ISP's server, the uploading username and password may be the same as your Internet username and password.

To publish, you need to know the following information:

- The server's address; for example, `http://www.server.com`.

- The uploading protocol used by the server; for example, HTTP or FTP.

- Any username and password that you are required to use to gain access to the server.

- The particular directory in which your files will be stored; for example, `http://www.server.com/ned/`.

Using a Publishing Utility

After your ISP provides you with instructions for uploading your files, you can make uploading easier by supplying those instructions to a Web publishing program like those built into FrontPage Express and Composer.

To use either of these utilities, first open the page you want to publish in the editor. Then, do one of the following:

- In Composer, click the Publish button and follow the prompts.

- In FrontPage Express, choose File, Save As to open the Save dialog box. In Page Location, type the complete URL the page will have on the Web. Click OK and follow the prompts.

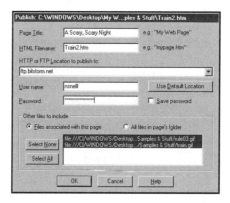

The first time you use one of these publishing utilities, you need to spend a few minutes supplying information about the Web server you'll use.

After you've done that, your uploads from then on will be quick and easy. These utilities remember all your server information, so after you enter the information once, you don't need to fiddle with it again; just start the publishing procedure as before, and most of the steps happen automatically.

Beyond Survival

Using FTP to Publish

There's a tried-and-true system for uploading and downloading files on the Internet called FTP (File Transfer Protocol).

FTP hasn't been covered yet in this book because it's a little tricky for beginners, and because you can use most Web browsers to download files from an FTP server, using the same steps you learned in Chapter 17, "About Files and Programs You Can Find." So until we came to this discussion of uploading, there was no need to get into FTP.

To find a
new FTP
client, use the
file-finding
techniques
from Part 5,
"Finding Other
Stuff," or
consult
Appendix B,
"Popular
Internet
Software and
Where to
Get It."

Some folks find uploading their Web pages to a server easiest
with an FTP client, when their ISP supports FTP uploads
(most do). Windows 95 and the Mac have their own built-in
FTP clients, but to use these clients, you must learn and use a
family of FTP commands.

A better choice is an easy-to-use graphical FTP client, which
combines the simplicity of a Web browser with the full power
of FTP. One popular choice for Windows, WS_FTP, which you
can get from

```
www.ipswitch.com
```

displays the directory of the FTP site you've accessed on the
right side of the window, and your computer's hard disk directory on the left. Downloading and uploading is easy:

- To download a file in WS-FTP, you drag it from the
  right to the left.

- To upload a file to a server, you drag a file from the
  left—your hard disk—to the right—the FTP server.

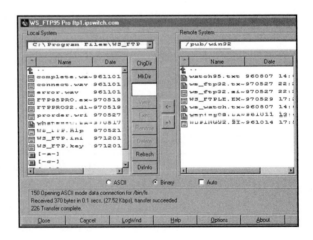

Cheat Sheet

The Trick to Fancy Messaging

Using Outlook Express, Messenger, or Collabra, you can send email and newsgroup messages containing all the objects and formatting you can put in a Web page—fonts, colors, pictures, backgrounds, and so on.

But to read the message with all of its formatting, your recipient must also use an advanced email or newsgroup program capable of displaying HTML-based messages.

Creating a Fancy Message

- In Outlook Express, open a new message window as you usually would. From the message window's menu bar, choose Format, Rich Text (HTML).
- In Messenger or Collabra, choose Edit, Preferences, then choose the Messages subcategory under the Mail & Groups category. Check the By default, send HTML messages check box near the top. Then close the Preferences dialog box and start a new message.

Composing and Formatting the Message

The message window of a fancy message shows the same tools as a Web-authoring program, so you can

- Compose and format an HTML message in Outlook Express exactly as you do a Web page in FrontPage Express.
- Compose and format an HTML message in Messenger or Collabra exactly as you do a Web page in Composer.

Using Stationery to Send Really Fancy Messages

Outlook Express includes a collection of "stationery," fun and funky backgrounds for messages. To create a message on stationery, choose Compose, New Message using, and then choose a stationery from the menu.

40

Creating Fancy, Formatted Messages

In Chapter 21, "Composing and Sending Email," you created email messages—wonderful, simple, flat email messages containing nothing but text. What you may not know is that you can put the same kinds of content and formatting you use in a Web page in an email message.

Basic Survival

The Trick to Fancy Messaging

You can send messages containing all kinds of fonts, colors, pictures, backgrounds, and links—if it can be put in a Web page, it can go in a message. There's one hitch to sending fancy messages like this: Your recipient may not be able to display them in their full glory.

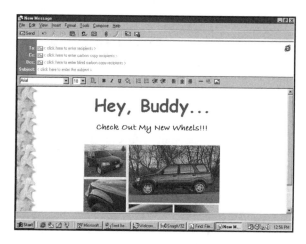

You can apply these techniques in both email and newsgroup messages.

Like a Web page, a fancy message must be created in HTML format. To read the message, your recipient must use an email or newsgroup program—such as Messenger or Outlook Express—capable of displaying HTML-based messages in addition to regular email messages.

Many of those using Internet email and newsgroups today cannot display HTML messages, so unless you happen to know that your intended recipient has an email program that can show HTML messages, it's often best to stick with plain text messages.

What Happens If I Send to Someone Who Can't See It?

What happens if you send an HTML message to someone whose email program can't show it? Nothing bad.

The text of your message still comes through fine (although it won't show formatting, such as fonts). In some cases, stray "garbage" characters may appear in your message when the recipient reads it, but the message will probably remain legible.

As long as your pictures or other formatting don't contain essential information, any recipient can get the substance of your message, if not its style.

Starting a Fancy Message

Pictures in your message become file attachments to the HTML-impaired email program, so recipients can open them in another program.

To create an HTML message:

- In Outlook Express: Open a new message window as you usually would. From the message window's menu bar, choose Format, Rich Text (HTML).

- In Messenger or Collabra: You must change the Preferences to send HTML messages. Choose Edit, Preferences, then choose the Messages subcategory under the Mail & Groups category. Check the By default, send HTML messages check box near the top. Then close the Preferences dialog box and start a new message as usual.

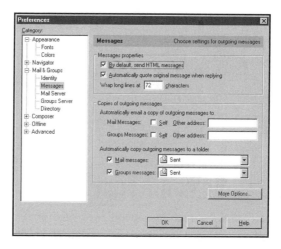

By default, most programs that can send HTML messages automatically send replies in the same format in which the message was received.

In other words, if someone sends you an HTML message (which means the sender's email program can display HTML), and you click Reply to respond to it, the message you create is automatically in HTML format.

Composing and Formatting the Message

When composing an HTML message in either program, you'll notice that the toolbar and menu bar show most of the tools and options available in the same suite's Web authoring program. Using the tools you see:

- You compose and format an HTML message in Outlook Express exactly as you do a Web page in FrontPage Express.

- You compose and format an HTML message in Messenger or Collabra exactly as you do a Web page in Composer.

When done composing and formatting, send as usual (refer to Chapter 21 for a refresher on sending email, if you need one).

Beyond Survival

Using Stationery to Send Really Fancy Messages

As part of its capability to support fancy messages, Outlook Express includes a collection of "stationery," fun and funky backgrounds you can use to dress up your messages.

To create a message on stationery, open Outlook Express and choose Compose, New Message using from the menu bar. A menu of stationery choices appears.

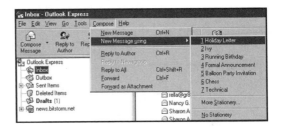

Choose a stationery, and then compose your message as usual. If the message already contains some sample text, you may edit or delete that text any way you like.

When finished, send the message as you would any other.

If the recipient's program can't show fancy messages, the text of your message still shows up— just without the fancy part.

PART

11

Appendixes

The appendixes contain information that's potentially useful. You get a directory of some cool Web sites and Web sites where you can obtain software. You also get some troubleshooting tips on surfing the net.

The appendixes include

- More Great Sites to Visit
- Popular Internet Software and Where to Get It
- When Things Go Wrong: Troubleshooting

A

More Great Sites to Visit

Arts, Culture, and Society

American Council for the Arts
www.artsusa.org

ArtsNet
artsnet.heinz.cmu.edu

ArtSource
www.uky.edu/Artsource

BooksOnline
www.cs.cmu.edu/
booktitles.html

Classical Music Online
www.onworld.com/CMO

Florida Museum of Hispanic and Latin American Art
www.latinoweb.com/museo

Internet Underground Music Archive
www.iuma.com

Jazz Online
www.jazzonln.com

The Louvre
www.paris.org/Musees/Louvre

Virgin Records
www.virginrecords.com

Ultimate Band List
www.ubl.com

Business

BizWeb
www.bizweb.com

CD Rate Scanner
bankcd.com

CNNfn (Cable News Network Financial Network)
www.cnnfn.com

CommerceNet
www.commerce.net

Dow Jones Interactive Publishing
bis.dowjones.com

The Economist
www.economist.com

Inc. Online
www.inc.com

Microsoft Investor
investor.msn.com

smallbizNet
www.lowe.org/smbiznet/

Wall Street Directory
www.wsdinc.com

Computer-Related Sites

Computer Systems

Apple Computer
www.apple.com

Compaq
www.compaq.com

Dell
www.dell.com

Digital Equipment
Corporation (DEC)
www.dec.com

Gateway 2000
www.gateway2000.com

IBM
www.ibm.com

Sun Microsystems, Inc.
www.sun.com

Toshiba
www.toshiba.com

Printers

Brother
www.brother.com

Canon
www.canon.com

Hewlett-Packard
www.hp.com

Modems

Hayes
www.hayes.com

Microcom
www.microcom.com

Practical Peripherals
www.practinet.com

Search Engines

Alta Vista
altavista.digital.com/

Excite
www.excite.com

Infoseek
www.infoseek.com/

Lycos
www.lycos.com/

Magellan
www.mckinley.com/

Open Text
www.opentext.com/

WebCrawler
www.webcrawler.com/

Yahoo!
www.yahoo.com

Government

FedWorld
www.fedworld.gov

Library of Congress
lcweb.loc.gov/

NASA
www.nasa.gov

The U.S. House of Representatives
www.house.gov

The U.S. Senate
www.senate.gov

The White House
www.whitehouse.gov

Education

100 Most Popular College and University Sites
www.100hot.com/college

College Board Online
www.collegeboard.org

Homeschooling Zone
www.caro.net/~joespa

Online Educational Resources
quest.arc.nasa.gov/OER

U.S. Department of Education
www.ed.gov

Entertainment/ Media

DirecTV (Digital Satellite)
www.directv.com

Roger Ebert
www.suntimes.com/ebert/ebert.html

Film.com
www.film.com

Mr. Showbiz
www.mrshowbiz.com

TV Guide
www.tvguide.com

TV Networks

ABC
www.abc.com

CBS
www.cbs.com

Cinemax
www.cinemax.com

The Disney Channel
www.disney.com/DisneyChannel/

ESPN
www.espn.com

Fox
www.foxworld.com

HBO
www.hbo.com

MTV
www.mtv.com

NBC
www.nbc.com

PBS
www.pbs.org

Movie Studios

MCA/Universal
www.mca.com

Metro Goldwyn Mayer
www.mgmua.com

Paramount Pictures
www.paramount.com

Sony Pictures
www.spe.sony.com/Pictures/
SonyMovies/index.html

20th Century Fox
www.tcfhe.com

Walt Disney Studios
www.disney.com/
DisneyPictures/

Warner Brothers
www.movies.warnerbros.com/

Health

Alcoholics Anonymous
www.alcoholics-
anonymous.org

Deaf World Web
deafworldweb.org/dww

Health World Online
www.healthy.net

World Health Organization
www.who.ch

Kid Stuff

Children's Literature Home
Page
www.parentsplace.com/
readroom/childnew/
index.html

Children's Storybooks Online
www.magickeys.com/books/
links.html

Clubs for Boys
www.worldkids.net/clubs/
boys.htm

Crayola
www.crayola.com

DC Comics Online
www.dccomics.com

Girlsworld Online Clubhouse
www.agirlsworld.com

Indianapolis Children's
Museum
www.a1.com/children/home.
html

Kid's Corner
kids.ot.com

News for Kids
www.newsforkids.com

Web Guide to Children's
Literature
www.ucalgary.ca/~dkbrown

Shopping Malls

Awesome Mall
malls.com/awesome

Cybermall
cybermall.com

Internet Shopping Outlet
www.shoplet.com

Magic Market
magicmarket.com

Shopping Utopia
shop-utopia.com

21st Century Plaza
www.21stcenturyplaza.com

Sports

AudioNet Sports Guide
www.audionet.com/sports

CNNsi (Sports Illustrated)
cnnsi.com

Golf.com
www.golf.com

Major League Baseball
www.majorleaguebaseball.com

National Basketball
Association
www.nba.com

National Football League
www.nfl.com

New York Yankees
www.yankees.com

Travel

American Automobile
Association
www.aaa.com

American Express Travel
www.americanexpress.com/
travel

Fodor's Travel Guides
www.fodors.com

Frugal Travel News
www.ftns.com

Internet Travel Network
www.itn.com

TravelNow Worldwide Hotel
Reservations
www.travelnow.com

World Travel Guide
www.wtg-online.com

B

Popular Internet Software and Where to Get It

Browsers and Other Client Programs

In your Web travels, on all sorts of pages, you will encounter little buttons with the Netscape or Internet Explorer logo on them, usually accompanied by the words "Download Now." Clicking one of these buttons takes you directly to the download page for the product.

Note: Addresses for the two most popular Internet client software suites—Internet Explorer and Netscape Communicator—are included in the following list.

Tucows Directory of Internet Clients
`tucows.mcp.com`

Cello (Windows)
`www.law.cornell.edu/cello/`
`cellofaq.html`

Client Software Directory
`www.w3.org/hypertext/WWW/`
`Clients.html`

Eudora Email
`wwweeudora.com`

Lynx (UNIX and DOS)
`www.cc.ukans.edu/about_lynx/`

Microsoft Internet Explorer 4
`www.microsoft.com/ie/`

NCSA Mosaic
`www.ncsa.uiuc.edu/SDG/`
`Software/Mosaic/`

Netscape Communicator (Navigator)
`www.netscapc.com` or
`home.netscape.com`

Plug-Ins, Helpers, and Other Browser Accessories

Adobe Acrobat Reader
www.adobe.com/

Macromedia Shockwave
www.macromedia.com

Microsoft Free Downloads
www.microsoft.com/msdown-load

Netscape Plug-ins Directory
home.netscape.com/comprod/
products/navigator/
version_2.0/plugins/

Plug-In Plaza
browserwatch.internet.com/
plug-in.html

Plug-In Gallery and Demo Links
www2.gnl com/ucors/ovamdla/

RealAudio/RealVideo
www.realaudio.com

General-Purpose Software Download Sites

Association of Shareware Professionals
www.asp-shareware.org

Children's Shareware
www.gamesdomain.com/
tigger/sw-kids.html

Download.com
download.com

Everything You Need to Surf the Net
www.primenet.com/~tcp

Kitty-Kat Software (Mac Stuff)
www.newc.com/kks

Shareware.com
shareware.com

Shareware Junkies
www.sharewarejunkies.com

Softword Technology
users.aol.com/shareware/
index.htm

Major Commercial Software Companies

Adobe Systems Incorporated
www.adobe.com

Apple Computer
www.apple.com

Borland
www.borland.com

Broderbund
www.broderbund.com

Claris
www.claris.com

Corel Corporation
www.corel.com

Electronic Arts
www.ea.com

FTP Software
www.ftp.com

IBM
www.ibm.com

Intuit
www.intuit.com

Microsoft
www.microsoft.com or
home.microsoft.com

Netscape Communications
www.netscape.com or
home.netscape.com

Novell
www.novell.com

Quarterdeck
www.quarterdeck.com

When Things Go Wrong: Troubleshooting

C

The information listed in this appendix is designed to help you through some potential trouble spots you might—I repeat *might*—encounter on the Internet. Remember, just because there are warnings here about some potential trouble spots does not mean you will experience any of these problems.

Q. I installed an Internet suite, but I can't find some of its components—such as its conferencing or Web authoring component. Is there another way to open them?

A. If the components aren't accessible, you may not have included them when you installed the suite. For example, when you install Internet Explorer 4, you have the option of selecting Minimal, Standard, or Full installation; only Full installs all components.

Try reinstalling (and perhaps redownloading) the suite, being sure to choose options for full installation.

Q. I have a 33.6Kbps modem, but my Internet connection dialog box says I'm connected at 28.8Kbps.

A. The speed at which a connection runs is determined by the slowest of the modems involved. If your ISP does not support 33.6Kbps access, you'll run at the ISP's modem speed (probably 28.8Kbps), no matter how fast your modem is. Some ISPs use different dial-in numbers for different speeds; contact your ISP and ask how to get 33.6Kbps access.

If you're already connecting through a 33.6Kbps modem at your ISP, your modem may be configured for 28.8Kbps operation. In Windows, click the Modems icon in Control Panel, and reconfigure your modem for its top speed. Consult your modem's manual for configuration details.

Also, note that a poor phone connection or a "noisy" phone line makes accurate modem communications more difficult. To compensate, most modems automatically slow down to a speed at which they can communicate reliably over the line. If you've eliminated the other potential causes, and you still see your modem communicating below its rated speed, you may have a noisy phone line. Contact your local telephone company to find out what can be done about the problem.

Q. I have a really fast modem, but I've noticed that downloads often happen much slower than the rated speed of my modem and connection. How can I download at full speed?

A. When a Web server sends you a file, it generally cannot do so all at once, and at full speed. The server must split its attention between sending you the file and taking care of other tasks for other users. Often, a download even pauses from time to time, and the speed of transfer is constantly going up and down. You can control the speed of your own connection, but there's nothing you can do about a slow server.

If it's a server you download from often, try accessing it at different dates and times, to find the time or day that it seems least busy—that's the time to download.

Q. I know that some programs, like Internet Explorer 4 and its components, are integrated with my computer's auto-connect capabilities so they can connect to the Internet automatically, when necessary. But sometimes, I get messages that I'm offline when I know I'm online.

A. Auto-connect works pretty well, but not perfectly—it's quirky. Sometimes while you're online, an Internet program may think you're offline. You can't really do anything to correct it, other than keeping up with new releases of your Internet software, in hopes that the problem gets fixed.

It's no big deal, however. If you're online when a program thinks you're off, when you try to do something that requires a connection, it asks whether you want to go online. Even though you're already online, just humor the program and click Yes. The program then immediately detects that you're online and continues the operation you started.

Q. Before I installed my browser, my graphics editing program opened whenever I opened an image file icon. Now my browser opens instead.

A. When you install most browsers, the installation program edits your file types Registry to make the browser the default program for lots of different file types, including Web page (HTML) files and most image file types. This is so the browser can display most types of files you encounter on the Web quickly, without having to open another program first.

If you want a certain image file type to always open in your graphics program instead of your browser, you can open your file types Registry and change the program used for opening that file from your browser to your graphics program. Alternatively, you can reinstall your graphics program, which may automatically update the file types Registry to make the graphics program the default for opening images.

If you do change the file types Registry, note that images that are part of a Web page layout—*inline* GIF and JPEG images —will still display in the Web page, in the browser. But if you click a link that opens an image file—even a GIF or JPEG file that's not inline—of a type

335

registered to your graphics program, the image will not appear in the browser. Instead, your graphics program opens to display the image.

Q. Sometimes when I enter a URL, use a favorite (or bookmark), or click a link, I get a message saying that my browser couldn't find the server or that it couldn't find the file.

A. When a browser reports that it can't find a file, it has successfully reached the server but can't find the specific file (page) the address points to. The file may have been deleted, renamed, or moved, or you may have typed the part of the URL that comes after the server address incorrectly. Try entering just the server portion of the URL—everything up to and including the first single, forward slash (/)—to access the server's top page, and then see whether you can navigate to what you want by clicking through links from there.

When a browser reports that it can't find the *server*, you may have typed the server address portion of the URL incorrectly. Or the server may have changed its address or gone out of business. However, when you get this message, the server may just be experiencing temporary technical problems. Double-check the URL, and if you still can't get through, try again in a few hours, by which time the server may be back in action.

Q. About half of a Web page, or only certain parts, appeared, and then everything just quit. My connection is still open—how do I display the rest of the page?

A. Sometimes, a Web page quits transferring to your computer midway through; it gets hung up somehow and quits. Most browsers feature a button labeled "Reload" (or "Refresh") that you can click to get the whole page all over again, from scratch. When a page seems incomplete or is acting quirky, Reload is often the first and best thing to try.

Q. When I click the Back button, nothing happens.

A. Is the Back button "grayed out"? If so, you've already reached the page at which your current session began. Back no longer works because there's nowhere to go back to.

If the Back button is not grayed out but seems to do nothing when you click it, you're probably looking at a page that uses frames. Remember, when you view a frames page, Back and Forward move you among the frames. If you keep clicking Back, however, you'll eventually move to the page you visited before the frames page.

Q. I've noticed that most Web server addresses begin with www. Is this a universal naming convention?

A. There is no hard and fast rule on using www. You've probably already noticed Web sites that vary, such as the Alta Vista search tool (altavista.digital.com) or Netscape's home page (home.netscape.com).

Some Web pages have *aliases* so a wrong URL leads to the right one. For example, many sites that don't begin with www nonetheless have an alias to an address that *does* begin with www. If you enter www.netscape.com, an alias at that address redirects you to the real page: home.netscape.com.

Aliases can bail you out when you enter an old or near-miss URL, but don't count on them; at Microsoft, www.microsoft.com and home.microsoft.com lead to two very different pages.

Q. If I choose to send someone an HTML email message, and the recipient is not using an email client capable of displaying HTML (like Messenger or Outlook Express), won't the recipient's email program just spit out the part it can't read?

A. Yes, that is true. If you receive a message containing HTML and your email client can't read HTML, the program ignores the part it can't understand.

That means you can send HTML email to anyone. But it also means that you must be sure that all important information in the message is contained within the text itself, and is not dependent on any images, text formatting, or other HTML features the reader will not see if his or her email program is not HTML compatible.

Q. My friend told me about this great newsgroup, but when I try to subscribe to it, I get a message that it's not on the server.

A. Does your friend use a different ISP or online service from you? Not all newsgroups are available on all servers. Some newsgroups are private and are maintained on servers accessible only to those with permission to use the newsgroup.

Also, each ISP maintains its own news server. Although most ISPs keep all newsgroups on their servers, some do not. For example, some attempt to minimize sexual traffic by not including the alt. groups on their servers. Others try to save space by including only newsgroups their members have requested. In case that's the reason you can't get through to the newsgroup, try sending an email to your ISP, requesting that the newsgroup be added to the server.

Q. I instructed my service provider's news server to display all newsgroups; I've been waiting for several minutes, and nothing seems to be happening.

A. Because of the sheer number of newsgroups on the typical news server, it may take several minutes to display all newsgroup names, so don't panic if it appears that nothing is happening. Just be patient. Also keep in mind that the speed of your Internet connection also affects how long it takes to display all those newsgroups.

Q. My friend called me up and said he visited my home page and that it looks sloppy. The text colors make it hard to read, he said, and the placement of graphics and text looks haphazard. The page looks okay to me in my Web authoring program, so what gives?

A. The same Web page looks different through different browsers. Some browsers handle certain kinds of formatting instructions differently than others, and some don't support certain kinds of formatting.

For example, some browsers don't support backgrounds, text alignment, or most image positioning options. When you've applied these techniques in your page, it will look dramatically different to someone using that browser than it does to you.

Variations in the viewer's equipment—such as different monitor resolutions (640×480, 800×600, and so on) or color depths (16 colors, 256 colors, and so on) may also play a role in making a page look different.

When you work on your page in a WYSIWYG authoring program like Page Composer or FrontPage Express, what you see is generally what you'd see if you viewed the page online through Internet Explorer (version 3 or 4) or any recent version of Netscape Navigator. Most folks online who use a graphical browser use either of these two browsers. Your tactless (but reliably frank) friend must be using a different browser. If you want to make sure your page looks great through any browser, keep the formatting simple, and test the page by viewing it through as many different browsers as you can get your hands on.

Glossary

address book   A feature in some **email** programs that stores your contacts' **email addresses** and other information for reference and to make addressing an email message easier.

authoring   The process of writing a **Web page**.

BCC (blind carbon copy)   When emailing, it is a way to send a copy of an email message without letting the other recipients know you are sending a copy.

Bookmark   **Navigator**'s method for letting a user create a shortcut back to a Web page the user will want to revisit. See also **Favorite**.

Boolean operators   These operators are designed to put conditions on a search to help make your search more specific. The most common Boolean operators are AND, OR, and NOT.

browse   To wander around a portion of the Internet, screen by screen, looking for items of interest. Also known as *surfing* or *cruising*.

browser   An Internet client that helps users browse, usually on the **World Wide Web**.

CC (carbon copy)   A copy of an email message, sent to someone other than the message's principal recipient.

certificate   A file used in secure connections to authenticate the server to a client.

chat   An Internet resource, sometimes also known as Internet Relay Chat (IRC), that allows two or more Internet users to participate in a live conversation through typing messages.

chat client   The **client** program required for participating in a **chat**.

client   A software tool for using a particular type of Internet resource. A client interacts with a **server** on which the resource is located.

Communicator   Also known as Netscape 4.0, it is the newest suite of Internet tools from Netscape Communications Corp. It includes a Web browser (**Navigator**), email (Messenger), newsreader (Collabra), Web authoring (**Composer**), and conferencing (Conference).

Composer   The Web authoring component of **Communicator**.

compression   The process of making a computer file smaller so that it can be copied more quickly between computers. Compressed files, sometimes called ZIP files, must be decompressed on the receiving computer before they can be used.

cookie   A collection of information that a Web server can leave on your computer for later access.

cyberspace   A broad expression used to describe the activity, communication, and culture happening on the Internet and other computer networks.

dial-up IP account   An Internet account, accessed through a **modem** and telephone line, that offers complete access to the Internet.

direct connection   A permanent, 24-hour link between a computer and the Internet. A computer with a direct connection can use the Internet at any time.

download   To transfer a file from a host computer to your computer.

email   Short for *electronic mail*. A system that enables a person to compose a message on a computer and transmit that message through a computer network, such as the Internet, to another computer user.

email address   The word-based Internet address of a user, typically made up of a username, an @ sign, and a domain name (`user@domain`).

emoticons   See **smiley**.

Explorer See **Internet Explorer**.

FAQ file Short for *Frequently Asked Questions file*. A computer file containing the answers to frequently asked questions about a particular topic.

Favorite **Internet Explorer**'s method for letting a user create a shortcut back to a Web page the user will want to revisit. See also **Bookmark**.

filter A system for automatically organizing and deleting selected email messages, such as **spam**.

flame Hostile messages, often sent through email or posted in newsgroups, from Internet users in reaction to breaches of **netiquette**.

form A part of a Web page in which users can type entries or make selections.

frame A discrete part, or "pane," in a Web page in which the screen area has been divided up into multiple, independent panes, each of which contains a separate document.

freeware Software available to anyone, free of charge (unlike **shareware**, which requires payment).

FrontPage Express The Web authoring program included in the **Internet Explorer** suite.

FTP Short for *File Transfer Protocol*. The basic method for copying a file from one computer to another through the Internet.

GIF A form of image file, using the file extension .gif, commonly used for inline images in Web pages.

helper programs Programs that run or show files that aren't part of a Web page and don't appear as part of the Web browser.

home page 1) The page a Web browser is configured to access first when you go online, or anytime you click the browser's Home button. 2) The main, or first, page displayed for an organization's or person's World Wide Web site (a.k.a, "top" page).

Hypertext Markup Language (HTML) The document formatting language used to create pages on the World Wide Web.

hyperlink See **link**.

imagemap In a Web page, an image that contains multiple **links**.

inline image An image that appears within the layout of a Web page.

Internet A large, loosely organized **internetwork** connecting public and private computer systems all over the world so they can exchange messages and share information. Sometimes casually abbreviated "the Net."

Internet Explorer A browser for the World Wide Web, created by Microsoft and available for free download from the Web and in a variety of software packages.

Internet Relay Chat See **chat**.

Internet service provider (ISP) A company from which you can obtain access to the Internet. This term is often used to distinguish the many companies that offer Internet access from **online services**, another kind of Internet provider.

internetwork A set of networks and individual computers connected so they can communicate and share information. The Internet is a very large internetwork.

intranet An internal corporate network, usually a local area network, that is based on Internet technologies, such as the use of Web browsers to display information.

IRC See **chat**.

ISP See **Internet service provider**.

Java/JavaScript Two of the programming languages used for writing **scripts** that enable advanced features in Web pages, such as some data collection and animation activities. The features added to a Web page with Java and JavaScript can be used only through a **browser** that's compatible with these languages.

link In a **Web page**, a block of text, an image, or part of an image that the user can activate (usually by clicking) to make something happen. Clicking links can jump the user to another Web page, start a program or **download** a file.

listserv   A program that automatically manages a **mailing list**.

log on   The act of accessing a computer system by typing a required username (or user ID) and password. Also described by other terms, including sign on/in, or log in.

lurking   Reading a **newsgroup** without posting to it, to study its culture.

mailing list   An online discussion group in which members share news and information through broadcasted email messages.

modem   A device that allows your computer to talk to other computers using your phone line.

multimedia   A description for systems capable of displaying or playing text, pictures, sound, video, and animation.

Navigator   The name of the popular browser sold by Netscape Communications Corp. It's available by itself, or within the **Communicator** suite. Navigator is often referred to casually as "Netscape," after its creator.

Net   See **Internet**.

netiquette   The code of proper conduct (etiquette) on the Internet, particularly when typing messages.

NetMeeting   A voice/video conferencing client included in the **Internet Explorer** suite.

Netscape   See **Navigator**.

network   A set of computers interconnected so they can communicate and share information. Connected networks together form an **internetwork**.

newsgroup   An Internet resource through which people post and read messages related to a specific topic.

newsreader   A **client** program for reading and posting messages on **newsgroups**.

offline   The state of being disconnected from a **network**.

online   The state of being connected to a **network**.

online service   A company such as America Online or CompuServe that offers its subscribers both Internet access and unique content available only to subscribers, but not to others on the Internet.

password   A secret code, known only to the user, that allows the user to access a computer that is protected by a security system.

plug-in   A program that increases the capabilities of a Web browser.

script   A program (sometimes external to a Web page, sometimes "embedded" as part of it) opened by a Web page to perform some special function.

search engine   A program that provides a way to search for specific information on the Web.

server   A networked computer that serves a particular type of information to users or performs a particular function.

shareware   Software programs that users are permitted to acquire and evaluate for free. Shareware is different from freeware in that, if a person likes the shareware program and plans to use it on a regular basis, he or she is expected to send a fee to the programmer.

shorthand   A system of letter abbreviations used to efficiently express certain ideas in email messages, newsgroup postings, and Internet Relay Chat sessions. Examples are IMO (in my opinion) and BTW (by the way). See Chapter 25, "Observing Proper Netiquette."

smiley   Character combinations used to express emotion in typed messages, such as email and newsgroup messages; for example, :-) is a smile. A.K.A. *emoticons* (emotional icons).

spam   Mass emailed material meant for promotion, advertisement, or annoyance.

streaming audio/video The capability of multimedia to begin playback as the file is being downloaded.

thread A series of **newsgroup** articles all dealing with the same topic. Someone replies to an article, and then someone else replies to the reply, and so on.

upload Copying a file onto a **server,** through a **network** (such as the Internet), from your computer.

URL Short for *Uniform* (or *Universal*) *Resource Locator*. A method of standardizing the addresses of different types of Internet resources so they can all be accessed easily from within a Web browser.

username Used with a password to gain access to a computer. A dial-up IP user typically has a username and password for dialing the access provider's Internet server.

Web See **World Wide Web**.

Web page A document stored on a Web server, typically in the file format HTML (.htm or .html). Web pages are retrieved from servers and displayed by Web browsers.

Web site A collection of World Wide Web documents, typically all on the same server, usually consisting of a **home page** and several related pages accessed from it. A site may contain any number of pages, from one page to thousands of interlinked pages and other files.

World Wide Web (WWW or Web) A set of Internet computers and services that provides an easy-to-use system for finding information and moving among resources.

worm A program that searches methodically through a portion of the Internet to build a database that can be searched by a search engine.

WYSIWYG (What You See Is What You Get) Refers to a program that shows you onscreen exactly the way a document will appear when published. For example, **FrontPage Express** and **Composer** show you a Web page you're creating exactly the way it will look on the Web to others.

ZIP file See **compression**.

Index

Internet Relay Chat (IRC), *see* Chat

Internet service providers, *see* ISPs

Internet software, 23-25

Internet suites, 26-27

Internet Explorer 4, 27-28
  Netscape Communicator, 26-27
  troubleshooting, 333

Internet zone, security systems (Internet Explorer), 100

investing online, 282-283

IRC (Internet Relay Chat), *see* Chat

ISPs, 35-36
  access numbers, 41
  billing options, 41
    Pay as You Go, 40
  choosing, word of mouth, 39
  comparing rates and plans, 39-40
  finding locally, 36
  modems, 42
  newsgroups, 43
  plans, unlimited access plans, 40
  software, 42
  startup fees, 40
  Web server space, 42

J-K

JPEG, pictures (Web pages), 298

junk mail, *see* spam

Kbps (kilobits per second), 16

keywords, *see* search terms

Kflex modems, 17

Kids Avenue Web site, 268

Kids Health Web site, 273

L

LDAP (Lightweight Directory Access Protocol), 167

libraries, on the Web, 6

links
  finding, 67-68
  imagemaps, 67
  images, 67
  practice using, 70-71
  text, 67

lists
  forms, 86-88
  Web pages, 297

Listservs
  businesses, Web presence, 289
  mailing lists, 205

Liszt Web site, 206

local access numbers, connecting to the Internet, 45

local intranet zones, security systems (Internet Explorer 4), 100

logging on, 45

lurking, chat rooms, 261

Lycos Web sites, 123

M

Mac versus PC program files, 152

Macmillan Computer Publishing's Design Resources Page Web site, 299

Macromedia Web site, 106, 111

Macs
  for Internet access, 19-20
  Internet access, setting up, 51

mailing lists, 9
  contributing to, 209
  email-only accounts, 32
  finding, 205
  Listservs, 205
  spam, 197
  subscribing to, 206-207
  subscription addresses, 205
  Welcome messages, 208-209

making calls, NetMeeting, 242-243

managing
  bookmarks, Netscape Navigator 4, 81
  favorites, Internet Explorer 4, 81
  history files, 82

media Web sites, 325

members, chat rooms, 248

memory for Internet access
  on Macs, 20
  on PCs, 19

messages

O

R

radio buttons, forms, 86, 88

ratings system, Recreational Software Advisory Council (RSAC), 275

reading
books on the Web, 6
news on the Web, 5
newsgroup messages, 225, 228

RealAudio player
plug-ins, 106, 110
Web sites, 106, 110

receiving messages, 189-190

Recreational Software Advisory Council (RSAC), ratings system, 275

replies, posting to newsgroups, 227

Reply to Author button, 227

Reply to Group button, 227

replying
to messages, 191-192
to newsgroups in private, 227-228

restricted sites zone, security systems (Internet Explorer 4), 100

RSAC, *see* Recreational Software Advisory Council

rules, *see* horizontal lines

running signup programs, 46-47

S

safety
Chat, 249
children, on the Internet, 268-271
online shopping, 280-281

sarcasm, netiquette, 212

saving
pictures, Web pages, 299
Web pages, 85

scaling pictures, Web pages, 299

scrambling secure sites, 86

scripts, 96
browsers, enhancing, 107

Search buttons
browsers, 124-125
Internet Explorer, 125-126
Navigator 4, 125

search engines, 121, 123-124
Web sites, 324
see also search tools

search terms, 135-136
versus categories, 129-130
multiple words, 139-140

search tools, 121
adding your sites, 291
databases, 122
people finders, 163
see also search engines

searches
controlling with operators, 140-142
hit lists, 136-137
improving success of, 137-139

search terms, 135-136

searching
for people, 164, 167, 169
people finders, 166
for Windows 95/98 programs, 157

secure sites, 91
identifying, 91
online shopping, 280-281
scrambling, 86
security systems, 91

security
customizing
in Internet Explorer 4, 96, 99-100
in Navigator 4, 96, 98-99
forms, 86, 89-90
see also privacy

security levels, changing zones (Internet Explorer 4), 101

security settings, zones (Internet Explorer 4), 100-101

security systems
Internet Explorer, Internet zone, 100
secure sites, 91

self-extracting archive file, 160

sending
email, 182
HTML messages to those who can't see it, 316
messages
at a later time, 182, 184
to more than one person, 184-185

wizards, Page Wizard,
301-303
word processors, creating
Web pages, 306
World Wide Web, *see* Web
writing
email, 181-182
messages in HTML, 317
newsgroups messages, 226
Web pages, tools, 297-298
WWW (World Wide Web),
see Web
WYSIWYG editors, creat-
ing Web pages, 303-304
WYSIWYG Web authoring
programs
Internet Explorer 4,
FrontPage Express, 298
Netscape Communicator,
Page Composer, 298
Web pages, 297

ZIP, 159
ZipIt Web site, 159
zones
security levels (Internet
Explorer 4),
changing, 101
security settings, Internet
Explorer 4, 100-101
security systems, 100
sites, adding, 100

X-Z

Yahoo!
People Search, 163-165
Web sites, 123, 206
Yahooligans Web site, 267